WHAT CAN I DO?

Ethics and the Situation

William F. Pray

Rhino Publications
Venice, California

Philosophy Library
Distributed by Rhino Publications
Venice, California, USA

What Can I Do/William F. Pray
Existential Philosophy
Includes bibliographical references and index

ISBN-13 978-1463637583
ISBN-10 1463637586
All right reserved
Printed in the United States

Table of Contents

PREFACE

I have designed this book as a pathway to accomplishing one of the most difficult human assignments imaginable: Change the world...or at least a part of it. Before you chuckle, wondering at the author's pomposity, and close up this little book to return it to the shelf, consider the fact that you have always wanted to do just that, change the world. This is not a guess. Everyone has dreamed of altering the events of history. Typically, this dream is quickly dismissed as the means to make any significant changes have forever eluded us, the little guys. Yet there is a way to save that dream and it is a method that has been around for as long as people have had the urge to alter the events of their time. There is nothing naïve, supernatural or religious about this method. It is a hard, practical, down to earth method to dramatically alter those very real, worldly circumstances that swirl about you. It is a method that can fit into every human experience, which makes this little book well worth the read.

Because of the nature of this project, this book is also a work of philosophy. After all, one of the more practical goals of philosophy has always been to change things. However, the work is not one written for the professional philosopher or the academic. This book will have the feel of philosophy without the academic structure with which the professional scholar is comfortable. This book, as the introduction will make clear, is aimed at the second or third year college student, that is, it is aimed at those individuals most likely to ask the question: What can I do? While a certain dose of philosophy is unavoidable, it is a philosophy for the layperson.

Additionally, because of the slight philosophical nature of the book I have provided ample everyday examples for the many theoretical discussions. I may be accused of going overboard in this regard, but given the widespread dislike and misunderstandings of abstractions it seems necessary. I might also be accused of slight redundancy as I have often tried to look at the same subject from many different angles. I hope this is looked on as a positive feature of the project.

This book is written in two parts, with the possibility programmed into the work that each part can be read separately. The first part, the more self-conscious philosophical part, is meant to support the second section. This part of the book is intended for those who insist, and rightfully so, on an ethical foundation for action, together with an analysis of that foundation. The second section is the more practical study for achieving the goal of change. This second section is the heart, the nuts and bolts of the work. As I said above, I have attempted to design this work so that the two sections can be read in either order, or independent of one another.

INTRODUCTION

Some time ago, at the invitation of a Professor of Philosophy, who was then teaching at an eastern university, I found myself speaking to a class of undergraduates on the topic of ethics. At one point I was laboring to convince the students that we all have a share of responsibility in all the events of the world of which we are aware. Further, I wanted the students to feel that they had a strong stake in all ethical behavior, ours, our neighbors, our political leaders, and indeed, in the behavior or people and political leaders everywhere. Unexpectedly, a student asked me a rather simple question: "What can we do?" she wanted to know. "I mean," she added, "okay, so you've convinced us that we have some share in responsibility, so, now what – what can I do right now about any of this?"

Her question was vital to my point, but frankly I only have the haziest recollection of what I said in response. I fear it was a rather weak reply, or at least, as I recall, unclear. However, I do remember being acutely bothered by the unresolved look on her face, a look that, as I struggled to answer her question, quickly turned to boredom. Later, I was persistently nagged by both her question and her look for some months. I found that I identified with the student, her question, and my inability to provide a clear and concise answer. After all, offering these students clear answers was what I was supposed to be doing there that day in the classroom.

Like many of us, I can recollect that time when I was a university student, that baffling time of my own rising anger and frustration. Like others in my place and time, I looked around me and saw many wrongs. Everywhere, it seemed, there was terrible injustice in a wilderness of suffering. It seemed to me, dramatically, that the gears of history were smelt of misery and pain, hammered with suffering and oiled with blood. These things have changed little, I think. The world reeked with ugliness then, and still does. I remember all too often wondering: What can I do about this? Students three thousand years ago must have wondered in puzzlement and asked the same question as we. Certainly, as the ancient Greek philosopher, Heraclitus, must have raised uncomfortable issues with his students, all those students that followed never stopped asking the same questions: What can I do? That student in that class that day came to me from a very long and distinguished lineage.

Therefore, there is no need to launch an introduction to this essay with trying to persuade anyone that there are multitudes of vicious horrors and wrongdoings in this world. One would have to be utterly unconscious not to be aware of these questions of injustice, so it is unnecessary to belabor the point with endless examples. Connecting ourselves to these wrongs is quite another matter, especially our connectedness in terms of personal responsibility. We seem abstracted by a ubiquitous sense of disconnect. This sense of disconnectedness is one of the two means by which personal responsibility is deflected. How does this come about?

First, it is extremely difficult to see in what way I, as one isolated individual, am even remotely connected to an issue in some far flung corner of the world, some place where I

iv

know no one, and have no serious thoughts concerning the events taking place there. It is certainly even more difficult to link myself *responsibly* in any personal way to those people and events. I am NOT responsible, I cry to myself. Yet some residual unease remains. These considerations have occurred to us all.

Second, should that primary deflection by denial fail, there is another and far less evident force at hand. That force is the idea-system which shelters me and provides me with a safe way to go about organizing my experience. I say the force is less evident because the idea-systems (or better understood as ideologies)[i] in which we exist and act are absorbed by us in a way similar to the way we breathe in air. From birth we are immersed in the dominate idea-system, considering it about as often as a fish considers the water in which it swims. We think and organize our world with these idea-systems, yet reflect on the nature of these systems hardly at all. In this project we will discuss and analyze ideology at great length. Prevailing idea-systems are not only what allows us to make sense of our world, but also allows us to make sense of our moral and ethical values and do so in a way that restricts access to the facilitating system itself. In other words, it is all but impossible to analyze the ideological system from our position within that system. Before analysis is possible, we must step out of one system and into another, or perhaps more than one – hardly an easy task. Consider that we barely recognize that our day-to-day ethical thoughts are guided by an idea-system not of our own making, but an inherited system fashioned by historical circumstances.

---

[i] As I will stress many times in this work, ideology is not to be confused with some political doctrine championed by political leaders. Correctly understood, ideologies are those idea-systems we use to offer meaning to our world, to the things and events that surround us.

Of all the systems of thought present in our world, the very idea of a system of thought itself, and the power of that system, is rarely recognized and studied at all.

A final comment: At some point it will occur to the reader that at bottom this is a book on ethics focused on *personal* ethics. One question will naturally arise. What of extending this personal ethical system to the socio-political sphere in general? Is such a thing possible? Is such a thing practical? On the surface of it the answer will appear to be 'No,' it is neither possible nor practical. I will maintain the opposite. With a few modifying considerations it is possible that this system of personal ethics can be extended society wide. However, that is a lengthy discussion and will have to wait for another project. This essay concerns itself with the individual and the personal ethical struggle we all face in confronting our world. It is my hope that this essay will contribute to a possible time when the bewilderment and the question of *what can we do* will be more easily understood and answered.

SITUATIONAL ETHICS[1]

The Situation

The Situation is the totality of our individual reality at any given moment. The totality of these Situational moments is arranged in three overlapping parts. The first part of the meaning of this totality is that it is shared by all of humanity. The second part of the total Situation is that it is particularized by historical forces. The third part of the total Situation is that it is individualized. The Situation is at the same time universal, particular, and individually unique. These claims need to be laid out through careful description.

The first part of the totality is the circumstance from which all else develops. That circumstance is the *primal* circumstance in which we first realize ourselves. There is less doubt about the truth of this primal circumstance than any other facet that emerges from it. This primal circumstance produces our most elementary fact: I am aware that I exist.[ii] Questions of how and why I exist are a whole other matter. Merely the fact that I can consider these other questions attests to the reality of my existence, which is to say that *I-am*.

Arriving simultaneously with this most elementary fact, the primal circumstance (i.e., *I-am*), is **the second part**, the *contingent context*, that is, the where and when I

[ii] The primal circumstance is also the source of many other unique and hopeful human features, such as, for example, imagination. Much more will be said about this later.

was flung into this world. It is from the tension between the *primal circumstance* and the *contingent context* that all human Situations are originally derived. The individual Situation is the momentary fluid circumstance of that derivative.

The contingent context presents the I-am with specialized questions. The nature of these questions can vary as vastly as the contingent context can vary. It is the unlimited nature of the argument between question and answer that engineers **the third part** of the totality, the uniquely individualized Situation.

For the individual, the most pressing of these questions will always surround issues of survival. These survival issues can emerge along physical, emotional and existential lines. [iii] Questions of threat and survival are sometimes obvious and sometimes they are disguised. Obvious or disguised, it is the tension inherent in these questions that develops and announces the human Situation. The tension found in the dialectic of the Situation (that is, as the individual confronts the contingent context) is always present and in one way or another must be resolved. The resolution creates a new contingent context which is felt as new tensions confronting the *I-am*. The tension must find a resolution, a resolution which establishes a new

---

[iii] Existential and existentialism as it is meant here is the fundamental fact of existence. The individual is alone and dependent on individual actions, freely chosen, *in so far as they are recognized and grasped.* The individual is solely responsible for those chosen acts that shape the individual's place in reality. This implies the complete freedom and the evolving possibility of the uncovering and recognition of those choices that alter the individual's position in total.

dialectical Situation, and so on. The force of this dialectic provokes three consequences for ethics.

The first consequence is that the human Situation is fluid and turbulent, ever evolving, with no final end in sight. This unrelenting ferment makes the assigning of universal ethical claims to the Situation extremely difficult and perhaps not at all possible in any meaningful way. We must remember to carefully distinguish between the momentary context, where ethical universal claims *appear* possible, and the total Situation itself, where such claims become destabilized by the *I-am* in argument with the tenacious equivocation inherent within the Situation.

The second consequence is that as the Situation is fluid, its effect on the individual is to cause that individual to continually alter position both intellectually and existentially. This is a derived Situation in which the individual passes relentlessly into new positions, vis-à-vis the contingent context in an ongoing and ceaseless process of uncovering and organizing. The individual stands on ambiguous ground and is thereby provoked into a continually altering position in the landscape. This ambiguous grounding is also to say the individual possesses the motive to freely *re-create* the self, both intellectually and existentially. As we will see, seizing those motives is one of the possibilities the primal circumstance offers to every individual.

And the third and final consequence is that the dialectic immediately *obscures* the importance of the primal circumstance, thus suggesting that the contingent context is primary. This means that both the impact of the primal circumstance and the manner in which the individual re-creates is hidden from view. This obscuring of the primal circumstance by the dialectical process adds a huge barrier to the evolution of the re-creating individual.

All three of these consequences (i.e., turbulent fluidity, evolving intellectual contingencies, and obscuring the true nature and impact of the *I-am*) have great importance for the question of ethics in the human Situation. Taken together we might choose to call the collected consequences *Situationism.* We need to take a closer look at this Situationism, which is to say take a closer look at the primal circumstance, contingent context, and the Situational dialectic. At this point an illustration will prove very useful.

Primal circumstance means that at any given time and place, for the *I-am!* the 'I' is basic. Contingent context is a specific time and place. So, for example, *I-am* in Wittenberg in 1637. The essence and the character of the 'I' is a variable of a context uncertain until the moment of the primal circumstance, the original flinging into this world. One possible derived Situation is that *I-am* a *Catholic* in Wittenberg in 1637. This last, being a Catholic in Wittenberg can easily be confused with the contingent context. It might be claimed that if the family, together with a sizable part of Wittenberg, is Catholic, therefore being a Catholic is part of the contingent context into which the individual is flung. This is not a correct inference. To be a Catholic is merely one possibility of many possibilities confronting the individual. By the middle of the 17th century there were many alternative Christian sects available, (Wittenberg being closely associated with Martin Luther), and also Hebrew and Muslim sects, not to mention the possibility of being a free-thinker. To be a Catholic is one of the choices possible to resolve the tension found in the interface between the primal circumstance and the contingent context. This was a choice and therefore a Situational event for the Wittenberg individual.

Consider also that it might also be claimed that the Wittenberg individual is a butcher, and this is so because the entire family is butchers. Consequently, is not being a butcher part of the contingent context into which the individual is flung? It should be clear that being a butcher is not an automatic part of the contingent context. Being both a Catholic and a butcher are choices in the evolving Wittenberg entity's Situation. This is a Situation derived from an interface of the *I-am* and the contingent context. In other words, just as being a Catholic [iv] is a choice so is being a butcher. What the contingent context does is present the individual with a host of contingent (dependent on the original flinging) possibilities. These possibilities may not be recognized by the individual of Wittenberg, but insofar as they exist, those contingent possibilities can pressure the individual, though they do not dominate the individual. It is always the existential *I-am* (i.e., primal circumstance) that dominates. From this interface a fresh Situation arises that becomes part of a new and evolving context. Situationism exists for the butcher of Wittenberg, 1637, as Situationism does for us today.

Like the human entity in the Wittenberg of 1637 we are all flung into a context which seems quite arbitrary.

[iv] The date of the illustration was not chosen arbitrarily. It lands our German butcher in the midst of a cataclysmic event, the Thirty Years War (1618-1648), a sweeping struggle wherein religion played a strong, influential role.

This first contingent context is the only context about which we have no choice. We might identify this flinging as the original or *inaugural* event. This original inaugural event places us in a context of established boundaries and strictures, (objective conditions, if you will) that present questions to the *I-am*, in this case the entity of Wittenberg. The questions are in the form of possibilities offered by the context. The energy, understanding and motivation that the Wittenberg entity brings to the question of these possibilities establishes completeness for the totality of the Situation. For us, as well as our human companion in Wittenberg, every inaugural event will present its own unique possibilities, the nature of which will ultimately afford unique solutions and consequences.

There is an important emerging conflict here. This is a conflict that will always exist between the *way* we are and *why* we are. This conflict and tension is the heartbeat of the human Situation. At the outset, the awareness of these unique possibilities will emerge from our deep unease over the nature of our primal circumstance. We suspect that we are all flung into a particular context for no particular reason about which we can be certain. This leads to an ache and an emptiness that provokes a kind of forlorn puzzlement, together with a vague fear that professional philosophers often refer to as an existential 'dread,' or 'angst.'[2] This free-floating sense of dread is different from ordinary fear in that we can point to no precise cause, nor does it ever go away entirely. This leaves us with a grave and uncertain sense of existential vulnerability, of being stripped of our foundation and held helpless and without meaning in the face of our own existence.

Secondarily, this sense of vulnerability must also be understood as part of a symposium of sensations extracted from our most basic of drives, our instinct to survive. This instinct to survive is not an ethical issue, or even a philosophical one; the instinct to survive merely is, and is forever running in the background. However, derivatives of this instinct to survive, when combined with the sensations of vulnerability provoked by free floating anxiety and dread, do have vast ethical implications. To know that we cannot survive life confronts us head-on, not only with our own physical vulnerability, but also with sneaking suspicions concerning a lack of purpose for our existence.

This sense of dread manifests itself at odd and unguarded moments, moments when we privately come to imagine that everything about us is somehow pointless, absurd, and nonsensical – including ourselves, and our very existence. It is not surprising that these thoughts come upon us most often when we are children, for only children have the minimal reaction to vulnerability and the fresh openness to entertain an unbiased reflection of the *I-am*. As we grow older, we are distracted from these primal issues by practical (and often not so practical) matters of existence – and perhaps we even desire to be distracted. We can be sure that our human companion flung into Wittenberg in 1637 felt the pain of this vulnerability and hollowness as surely as do we. As we will see, the entwining of these physical and existential vulnerabilities are deciding factors of Situational ethics.

In a way similar to any common household neurotic anxiety, we long to be rid of the pain that accompanies the psychic tension. The pain produced by neurotic anxiety can feel the same as this existential dread. We are filled with the need to be rid of the tension and the dread, push back against the foreboding with the belief that our being flung into a seemingly arbitrary context is explainable by some unknown, but deliberate purpose. We are flung at the will of the gods, or the real meaning of the primal circumstance is found in the alignment of the stars, or that our sense of purposelessness only comes upon us because we are actually the creature of mad thoughts in the mind of a mad playwright. If design and meaning are not ready at hand we will dodge the bullet by creating a meaning of our own and thus give us an ideological platform (no matter how shaky) to stand upon. Yet, in the end, and beset by our ability to reflect, any explanation concerning our having been flung into this-or-that context is compromised by the doubt and fear that inevitably creep in around the edges of our cleverly constructed sense of meaning.

Reflection is both a blessing and a curse. With reflection comes a terrifying consequence. We come not only to suspect that there is no cause, no meaning behind the *I-am*, but also that there is no design, no plan for the future of the individual. About the reflection on the *I-am* in-the-moment we can be certain. I think, therefore I exist, per Descartes. But about the meaning of all else, both before and after, there must always be a measure of doubt and mistrust. It is within this dark cloud of doubt and mistrust that we find a silver lining. It is within the foundationless individual that we uncover a principal source of two positive and original features of our human uniqueness, features that combine to form a source of hope. This is not a way out of the dread of meaningless, but a way to cope with it, a way to co-exist, and a way to achieve personal peace down a path toward achieving a re-creation of the self.

The first original feature of our uniqueness is that this dread inspired tension provides an inexhaustible source of energy needed to fire the kiln for the Situation. It is the wellspring for the inexhaustible restlessness inherent to our species. This energy from the angst we can neither outrun nor outspend. It is the source of the energy that propels our will and our drive to create, as well as our drive to destroy.

The second original feature is that this anxiety is a pointed 'tell' for a uniquely human fact derived from our primal circumstance: *If there is no meaning, there are no boundaries to freedom*. To the best of our knowledge, no other creature on this earth is beset with this dread of meaninglessness. Consequently, for no other creature does there exist a Situation. And for no other creature does there exist anxiety over the fact of freedom.

This second feature – our personal and boundless freedom – facilitates our seeing the contingencies inherent within the context. Once understood, these contingencies aid us in making those choices that will inevitably confront the individual. Together, these features launch us into creating and re-creating our uniquely human and uniquely individual Situations, that is, those contingent contexts with which we must endlessly, Situationally struggle.

Following the primal circumstance – the original flinging into this world – all of the other emergent contexts seem to shed, to one degree or another, the feel of the arbitrary, the questionable, and the uncertain. Our choices, provided by the contingent context – even those choices of which we are less than fully conscious – restructure Situations that will evolve into some new context. Of course, with the arrival of the new context we are once again bound to become anxious and fearful, thus pressing us forward to face new choices and emerging Situations, evolving into yet a new contingent context. In a manner of speaking, the original flinging provides us with both the means and the ends for contingency. Let us return to the butcher of Wittenberg.

The Catholic butcher having been flung into the context of 1637 confronts a most obvious contingent context, the Wittenberg of 1637. This world of 1637, this context, represents a large portion of the objective limitations for our butcher's Situation, limitations about which it might seem that little can immediately be done. But it also presents the butcher with a host of contingencies. The fiery energy of the flinging still lingers. The ascendant question becomes one of how clearly does the butcher grasp the contingencies of the Wittenberg context? Pertinent is to ask about the butcher's level of experience? The means are at hand – the energy of the flinging – but what of the ends of freedom? In other words, rather than see only the objective limitations arising from having been flung, does the butcher clearly see all the contingencies? This 'seeing' is the first clue to bringing about a change in the butcher's Situation. The 'seeing' represents the level of experience growing at the heart of Situationism.

Just what is it that the butcher can grasp? Can the butcher fully grasp what is most important – that within the limitations and strictures of the context, there is no blueprint to follow – that there is no plan for a new, developing context? Can the butcher see that the means, the primal circumstance, do not simply allow for the ends of freedom, but demand freedom? This 'seeing' is partly an issue of experience, and partly a problem for analysis, with both experience and analysis so interwoven that they generally are lumped together under the heading of what we usually call 'knowing,' or as a history of personal experience – in this case we refer to the butcher's personal storehouse of 'knowing'.

What we see and what we recognize can move us forward from what we experience toward what we 'know.' To 'know' can decidedly alter our relationship to the contingent context and do so almost immediately. For example, imagine that a loved one needed a kidney transplant. Would we consider being a donor? In today's world this is not so fantastic a proposition. Many of us would unhesitatingly say yes, for the human Situation tells us that saving the life of a loved one would override nearly any other consideration. However, let us suppose that we can somehow come to know that our kidney recipient would walk out of the hospital and die in a car accident only a week following the transplant operation. Armed with this foresight, this sudden blast of knowledge, would most of us not back away from being a donor? This is an extreme example, of course, and a fanciful one, but it does illustrate how knowing can and does suddenly alter our relationship with experience and the contingencies of our context, changes the content of our context, if you will, and thus realigning our choices.

Given this, how might the butcher affect the objective limitations by a clear grasp of the context, that is, by a fundamental *Situational analysis* of the contingency inherent within the context as it confronts the butcher? Any failure to have a clear grasp (Situational-analysis) of the contingencies found in the (or any) context obviously represents strong limitations to any new, emergent context. The exercise of freedom is dependent on both truth and knowledge.

Regressively, human experience and contingency are ultimately dependent on the original and foundationless *I-am.* This is to say that the Catholic butcher in the Wittenberg of 1637 owes a first dependence to the primary circumstance. For to already say the 'Catholic butcher of Wittenberg' implies a fully developed Situation. We can probably assume that our citizen of Wittenberg became a Catholic and butcher out of some inheritance derived from the inaugural event. To choose the tools-at-hand provided by the context and the prevailing ideology[v] is the line of least resistance. Butchery might well have been the family trade, Catholicism the family religion – and thinking analytically and rationally demanded intellectual tools not

---

[v] Again, I must stress that ideology must not to be confused with political doctrine, as is very often done. To reiterate, by 'ideology' we mean those prevailing system of ideas by which we organize the experience of our reality with the intent of giving it meaning. Ideology is a platform constructed of ideas upon which we stand in order to survey and organize what we see and feel. These idea platforms are not constructed by individuals or groups of individuals. The best and most general way to think of ideology is that ideology arises by historical conditions posed in the form of questions being answered by groups of individuals. The answers form the idea platforms by which we solve and understand the historically posed questions. As the historical conditions change so do the answers to these changes, and so the ideologies change.

readily found within the context or the ideological matrix interlocking the Wittenberg experience of 1637. In a manner of speaking, we might say that the butcher's 'hard-drive' worked exactly as does anyone's, at any time in history (and prehistory), but the arrival of sophisticated 'soft ware' was as yet somewhere down the time line, and dependent on the development of more adequate programming (i.e., the arrival of a new ideology).

Even granting these limitations, the Wittenberg butcher can bring some measure of control over the developing Situation. Although the butcher has objective limitations on choice, as do we all, yet even within these restrictions the context contingently provides tools. If these tools are uncovered and properly engaged they can bring about alterations in the relationship between subjective experience and objective circumstance which will ultimately develop into the butcher's Situation. We might say that each of us, like the butcher of Wittenberg, has the greatest control over the objective circumstance through our subjective evaluation. We might say that by virtue of the *I-am*, we are masters of the *I-am*. This control of over how we manage our experience with the objective world, and how that experience, that knowing, is organized and evaluated, determines to a large extent our Situation. Our knowing (or perhaps our not-knowing) is the greatest challenge we face, but be assured that our knowing is also the choice-changer with which we can make over our contingent context. This in turn alters our relationship with the objective world and the individual's evolving Situation.

It is well within the control of the Wittenberg butcher to manipulate the experience of the contingent context. By uncovering and seizing elements found within the context the relationship between the subjective and objective are affected and the living Situation altered. For example, should the butcher choose to do so, the contingent context of 1637 has presented the butcher with the experience of printing and literacy. This does not mean the butcher *is* literate, but rather that the butcher can *choose* to become literate and thereby radically recreate the Situation. Admittedly, for the butcher in 1637 this will be accomplished with considerable difficulty as books were not widely available, public schools nonexistent, and tutors expensive. Obstacles seem formidable, *as they always do*, to everyone, everywhere, *but never insurmountable.* One small, but difficult, step – reading, will forever recreate the 'knowing' relationship between the butcher's Situation and the objective, contingent context, and therefore radically transpose the context and consequently the Situation.

This transposition of context generates a secondary consideration issuing from a reflection on the *I-am*. Exactly how much are we really in control of our own destiny? Can we be truly masters of our own fate? We must ask the question: Is not the objective baggage of cultural, historical, economic, and psychological con-ditioning so overwhelming that it puts the freedom of will, upon which mastery over our fate demands, out of bounds; free will is only a foolish myth. Would the butcher even *think* to learn to read? Is not the butcher's conditioning by context already so paramount that the necessary *freedom* to choose is an illusion? Is not determinism a truly objective limitation – just exactly how 'free' is the individual?

There are two answers to this question. The first is existential. Our primal circumstance clearly dictates that freedom is the only condition that is beyond choice. We are free by dint of our groundless existence. We are condemned to freedom. There is just enough of the resplendent in this answer that it begs for something worldlier, which leads to the second, more practical answer. We can reference and cross reference causation and beat ourselves endlessly with questions over the boundaries and limits to free will. We can hamstring our motivation over determinism verses indeterminism or some combination of the two, (usually referred to by professional philosophers as *compatibilism*) and throw up our hands in despair. We may anguish over these things all we want, but at the end of all this torment, and despite the fact of uncertainty, utility will take hold and we will all *behave* as though our actions were a product of free will. To paraphrase Kant, when making up one's mind one cannot, at the same time, consider the decision already predetermined. We must make up our mind about a decision.[3]

Like the butcher, there are always objective limitations to our action; there are always pressures that hamper our designs, unconscious psychological conditioning that seems to turn freedom into pathos and free will into cliché. Such limitations have occurred to us all. Yet even with these issues in mind, and thinking within the scope of objective limitations, and mindful of the pressures, we carry on as though we all make *apparently* free choices, and thereby hold ourselves accountable for these choices. Despite all our suspicions surrounding the truth of free will, we act as though we do have a considerable measure of freedom and free will. It is hard to imagine living in a practical world with any other outlook.

To illustrate: We can say that it is highly improbably that our 17th Century, Catholic butcher in Wittenberg would ever have had the experience of flying. This is one of the objective limitations found within the context confronting any person of 1637. It follows that as such an experience is not within the realm of the butcher's contextual awareness, so such an opportunity will not be missed, much less be entertained as a possibility for free choice. The same thing cannot be said for reading. The awareness of reading was relevant for the butcher in 1637 – had not the butcher seen a printed bible? It surely *occurred* to the butcher to learn to read. Of the objective conditions which make up the butcher's contingent context, reading is one. Clearly, reading would recreate the 'knowing' (i.e., the subjective condition) and this would also generate a complete transformation of the butcher's context. None of this in any way settles the issue of free will verses determinism, but it does strongly suggest that freedom is a function of the changing relationship between subjective and objective conditions. At the same time, it does not deny that freedom, while a creature of contingent context, is rooted in the primal circumstance of all individuals. Free will and determinism are very real actors in an ongoing dialogue, but they also appear to be players whose roles change in the changing realm of the Situation.

To sum up, barring insanity, the *I-am* is the primal circumstance, a fact about which we ought to doubt the least. Therefore, the original *I-am* is bound by that primal circumstance to contingent context. It is the inaugural event surfacing in the original contingency that conjugates all the contextual possibilities tendered by existence of the primal circumstance – the *I-am*. In a way, if the *I-am* is correctly grasped it can be seen as the 'set-up' for all the various Situations that are to follow from its flinging into some contingent context. Situationism is born of the impact of the flinging against the contingent context that insists on a freely chosen re-creation of the *I-am*.

It is from this inaugural event, and the primal circumstance, which we can both embrace and attempt to escape, that we develop a sense of certainty of experience upon which all our actions are predicated. We may wish to resist the certainty (and truth) of the responsibility for our evolving re-creation. Such a resistance typically takes the form of an escape from the truth of our individual Situation through adhering to some form of deterministic philosophy. For example, we can manufacture some grand spiritual ideology, or wallow in some pseudo-scientific system of genetic predisposition around race. Such idea-systems are intended to create distractions which have at least the result of avoiding a direct confrontation with meaninglessness and the freedom it implies.

Strangely, what human freedom really demands is the embrace of human meaninglessness. We must stabilize certainty and truth within a greater context of meaninglessness. It is this last, the experience of meaninglessness, and its effect on the evolution of certainty and truth, which best serves to impart understanding to the ethics of human actions.

Certainty

When we ask: *What Can I Do?* we ask about both the Situation and action. When carrying out an action intended to have positive results for others around us, we consider the 'rightness' of the action. This thing, this 'rightness,' raises the specter of ethics. Therefore, to begin with action is to begin with ethics, or rather an oxymoron: *ethical certainty*. This oxymoron is partially due to the dynamic of action within the Situation, but is mainly due to the truth of certainty. We will first look into certainty – and then truth – as it is those things of which we are certain to be true that make up the supporting struts for any Situational platform concerning the rightness of deeds.

We draw our sense of certainty from the manner in which we organize our experience. There is really no other way to state this. In a rather simplistic way, purely rudimentary certainty requires elementary organization of experience often characterized by little more than a one-to-one correspondence. For example, I can say that I am certain that my hands are typing the keys which control the words emerging on this page. This sense of certainty arises because I have never had the experience of other hands at the ends of my arms so I continue to type, quite certain that these are my hands and not another's. I can wonder, am I certain that there is a closed door to my right? Should my daughter call me, I would open the door, rather than try to walk through it. I have never experienced a door that I could walk through. Further, I can say that one pencil on my desk and another pencil indicate that I have two pencils on my desk. I can abstract this experience to one X and another X equals two X's, and this experience will always bear the same result. My experience in these regards is simplistic and universal, and so the conclusions have the *feeling* of certainty. Of course, any resulting abstractions can be easily generalized.

Such rudimentary experiences have led some philosophers to conclude that certainty follows behind the obvious truth of an experience.[4] Yet we realize that not all propositions and actions are as obvious and prosaic as opening doors or the addition of one plus one. This realization greatly complicates matters surrounding both truth and certainty. Rather than certainty following truth, it may be, as will be argued here, that truth is a thing we bring into the world by the certainty of organized human experience.

Many actions, particularly political or social actions, are acts on a far different scale than the elementary notions mentioned above. These represent actions that sweep up huge masses of individuals, sometimes plunging them into utterly catastrophic events. Here the vitality of uncertainty lives and breathes and should take the co-pilot's seat in decision making – and sometimes the pilot's seat. The very best of the world's leaders might appear certain of their actions, but privately these leaders, at least the very brightest of them, retain a healthy sense of uncertainty, for to doubt means to think. It is also here that the organization of experience becomes more knotty and multifarious. Experience as the cornerstone to certainty no longer easily rides some kind of one-to-one correspondence, but rests on organizational patterns of far greater depth and complexity. As we will see, support for these patterns requires acquired ingredients.

As there are few actual differences between the mind of public and private figures, so uncertainty is the same with all individuals. It is with us individuals that the obvious benefit brought by doubt and uncertainty emerges most clearly. It is because of doubt and uncertainty that we are required to stop, reflect and consider, and do so very carefully. Without the doubt and uncertainty that provokes thinking, the stuff that goes on in our head would be indistinguishable from the synaptic firing of a dog or a cow. This is why doubt and uncertainty form (or at least should form) a main pillar of ethical action, and not just with world leaders.

Uncertainty seems to increase as we relate to other human beings. The more intense the action or interaction with others the greater should be the intrusion of uncertainty. It seems obvious that actions with or about other humans seem more inherently uncertain than the material objects in our world. If I bend down to pick up a stone then toss it, saying: 'I have thrown the stone,' it seems hardly worth the time to question the certainty of the act. This goes back to the elementary, one-to-one correspondence. Of course, we could always say that we have dreamed that we tossed the stone, and so forcibly interject doubt – but then we could say that we are dreaming that we are dreaming, and so on, a regression which begins to sound increasingly foolish. No, we proceed as though tossing the stone is a certainty. Not so in the interaction with others. Interactions with others involve certainties and uncertainties along a much different experiential line. They insist on different reflection based on different patterns of organization.

As we create experience with our actions, these experiences flow behind us, into the past, become part of the settled, the fixed, or as we might say, a fact! So it would seem that the past is more certain than the present, but is this really so? In the personal sense of creating an experience, the answer is apparently yes. If I shoot myself in the foot and cripple myself for life, this is a creation of personal history, the certainty of an experience which I cannot seem to escape. I must live with this created fact for the balance of my life. But historical experiences are less certain. It seems a settled fact that there was a Battle of Waterloo in June of 1815. However, just as there are those who believe that the moon landings were all staged on a Hollywood movie set, or that Auschwitz was built by grips in an effort to give Jews worldwide sympathy in their struggle for a homeland, there is the possibility that this Battle of Waterloo could also be a myth, an elaborate hoax concocted by politicians and journalists to establish the invincibility of the British Empire. Uncertainty can be cast on historical truth, if only for the reason that others have created the experience which generate the certainty.

The meaning of 'the others' has far reaching implications which will be explored later. At this point it is only important to note that external objects, such a book or a stone, have less uncertainty attached to them than my actions related to these objects. When I see a stone in my yard or a book on my shelf, I am not likely to ask myself, "Do I really see the stone or the book?" However, if I were to toss the book onto a fire and burn it, or throw the stone against a neighboring house, the act forces my cognition to come into play. It is clearly possible to question the certainty of my action, especially in regard to motive and causation. A much stronger sense of uncertainty is aroused when we witness others burning books, or throw stones against houses. The rise of uncertainty provokes serious puzzlement with facts and truth. Do I really see what it is that I see? A degree of incredulousness is kindled because even though we witness the action, we cannot be certain at all of why others are doing anything. The level of uncertainty (and puzzlement) grows even higher when we are told about people a hundred years ago burning books and throwing stones at buildings. What are the real facts? What was their intent? Can we ever know? Can we ever really be certain of the truth?

The most pertinent of questions is to ask: How can we arrive at any state of certainty, especially regarding the material reality beyond my own self? Is universal certainty in any regard possible, and if not what does that say about truth and ethics? If I were to say that a human being has never walked on the moon I would be the butt of hoots and smirks about the state of my mind, or questions about my whereabouts since nineteen-sixty-nine. I could argue, as suggested above, that walking on the moon was all a stunt, fabricated on a soundstage in Hollywood. The event never really took place at all. I – as the 'other' – am injecting doubt. But in so doing I will also begin to doubt. So a *decision* must be made by me and the others. Based on patterns of organized experience I *must decide* on certainty. The real question then becomes one of how do we min-imize uncertainty, or raise the level of certainty and thereby avoid the possible arbitrariness in our actions? In other words, is there some rule we can follow to make the decisions we must make concerning certainty?

Consider that there must be a particular application of the experience we have acquired and organized with what we see as it entwines with intentional behavior. Certainty, and its relationship to the truth of the Holocaust, for example, is a far more difficult matter than the truth of my fingers waving before my face. As events gather in the dust of history, the stability of certainty becomes ever more difficult to maintain. As in the case of any historical event, such as the Battle of Waterloo or the Holocaust, the shrouds of myth and distortion can interfere with our clear and certain sight of the action or event. It is entirely possible that ambitious people could have fabricated the evidence for the Holocaust – or is it? How we organize our *experience* becomes the tell for truth. We must reflect on intent, and that reflection demands that we must organize our experience in such a way as to consider the scope, the size, cost and the expense of human energy demanded by such a hoax. Here patterns of organization prove to be a linchpin in decision making. It is our manner of organizing experience, in this case concerning human intent that ignites doubt, and also provokes the urge to pause and reflect. The breath of our organized experience – that is, what and how we have studied of 'the other,' – will set serious boundaries for our grasp of human intent and therefore guides us to both a good decision on certainty and an insightful decision on truth. Quite simply, the certainty of every truth seems to hinge not so much on what we have uncovered, but on how we have *cognitively organized* what we have uncovered about the nature of our world.

Now emerges the most vital of the ingredients. This organization of experience implies organizational tools, tools that we typically put under the ultra-vague heading of thinking. However, thinking is based not so much on what you have uncovered, that is, raw experience, as it is based on the way in which we have *chosen* to cognitively organize the uncovering of your world. It is with that choice of organizational tools that the elements of both certainty and uncertainty arrive. We can frustrate certainty through poor choices in organizational tools, possibly through the adaption of one of the numerous pre-existing templates for any type of organized arrangement of experience. For example, in our modern world we have come to realize that attempting to organize experience using some template of the supernatural or of superstition can lead to profound and egregious errors. To illustrate: If our experiential organizing arrangement includes magic, then the construction of Auschwitz and the other trappings of the Holocaust for the purpose of hoodwinking humanity becomes entirely feasible. Much truth depends on the templates used for organizing experience.

To better handle this particular aspect of understanding, we will call the various organizational frameworks some form of *ideology*,[vi] (a topic about which a great deal will be said throughout this project). Ideology, that is to say, the arrangement and adjustment of experience through patterns and systems of ideas, are templates we

---

[vi] The prevailing system of ideas by which we organize and mediate the experiences we uncover in our reality. We might say that ideology *intends* to give human experience meaning.

must choose. Within limits it is difficult to avoid the conclusion that we organize experience through our choice of one system of ideas over another. Our decisions concerning certainty and eventually truth are grounded in our choice of a template of ideology. An uncomfortable bottom line in all of this is that we choose what to be certain about. Ultimately, then, it would seem that we choose what truth we will bring into the world.

It is through our understanding of what is true and what is false that we can and do make the ethical decisions that foundation nearly all of our actions. Considering the above, it seems that as ideology underwrites certainty, and certainty underwrites the truth of our actions, then ideology underwrites all our ethical actions. Our personal idea platform then emerges as the central theme in the assessment of ethics. This connection of our chosen idea platform, as the organizing principle behind certainty and truth, may not be at the forefront of our thoughts, but a moment of reflection will reveal that without some sort of organizational tool behind our choices we cannot make a decision between choices that would lead to good or bad consequences. If it is accurate to say that nothing is beyond the templates of ideology, then it seems to follow that absolute truth must also lie beyond our grasp and therefore all our decisions become threatened to some degree by ambiguity. This consideration alone can – and should – soften the often stubborn resoluteness of human actions.

What this boils down to is that in ways we do not ordinarily consider, what we are certain about and what remains for us as uncertain is largely a function of our choosing an ideology. With our choice of an idea platform as our only guide, we ultimately choose about what to be certain and what to doubt. [5] Therefore, within a very careful understanding of the nature and meaning of who and what we are, and how we came to stand upon one idea platform as opposed to another, we can say that we are free to choose certainty and truth. We might even go so far as to say we are condemned to freely choose the organizational process we employ to bring certainty and truth into the world. Obviously, in saying that we have this freedom to choose the organizing process, it follows that particular Situations can arise having profound implications for range of choice in the process, and therefore for the actions themselves.

In passing, we should note that it is best to resist the temptation to substitute the concept of probability for certainty. Probability suggests quantification and scientific rigor. I wave my hand in front of my face and ask, how certain is it that those fingers are really there and are mine? How can we quantify such a question as this, or apply scientific analysis? We cannot. Certainty, rather than pro-bability, is the better concept in many cases involving truth, and much better in the consideration of ethics.

Our choice of an ideology clearly bears a symbiotic relationship with truth. Ideology draws much of its authority from past certainties concerning truth, while our past choosing of certainty buttresses the truth of our mainframe ideology. This little dialectic is one major source of the uncertainty we feel when considering the ethics of our actions. Are we seeing and understanding our world as it truly is, or have we chosen to be misled, or chosen in some way to act by false witness? Of course, by choosing an ideology, our position on certainty enters the realm of contingency. The force of our choosing and idea system is ever present and ever ready to toss a monkey wrench into the workings of truth and, eventually, ethics.

Truth

Our actions, good or bad, right or wrong, are largely based on our understanding of truth. Yet, don't we all tend to ignore questioning truth, that is, do we not commonly by-pass a clear understanding of 'truth' and speak around truth as though we have some immediate or intuitive understanding of what is truth – its nature, even its infallibility? Writers, including professional philosophers, quite naturally show a tendency to assume the truth-value of their subject. There is nothing unusual about this. In a way, doesn't every thought take for granted its own suppositions? It is difficult to seriously discuss a subject without supposing its truth. Unfortunately, this tendency can stir up quite a few misunderstandings which often lead people to talk right past one another. To avoid this we ought to spend a moment or two discussing this thing called truth with special regard to its impact on our subject.

Some statements seem so obviously certain that we are inclined to shuck the truth of them off as too ridiculous to ponder. We can say that I pick up a stone from the ground. Then add that is it not a fact that there is a stone in my hand? And further, is it not true that the stone in my hand is the one I picked up off the ground? It is this type of obviously true statement of fact we might throw off as blatantly certain – this statement of objective fact. But notice how we have almost automatically run the idea of truth and fact together, blurred them as though one were synonymous with the other. We do this countless times, because at first glance it would seem that what is 'true' is also a statement of which we are certain – a *true, objective fact*! Closer scrutiny will show that there is an important distinction to be made here. This distinction is based on something other than questions of certainty, *per se*, and entails its own consequences for our project.

To get a precise handle on this distinction between truth and fact, let us ask a question which is not so obvious: Is the stone in my hand an objective reality (i.e., a fact), or is the stone merely a meaning-thing in my mind, that is, a thing that has meaning (or *substance*) only in my mind? This question is not simply the interjection of doubt, but the positing of an alternative understanding of the stone, that is, an alternative understanding of its meaning as fact. The stone just might be *both* a meaning-thing in my mind and a real thing existing out of mind. Said this way, such a characterization seems not so earthshaking, and a con-clusion that has occurred to a great many,[6] but it will take us to consequences not seen at first glance.

Consider the stone. It seems clear enough that the stone possesses some kind of objectivity that is separate from the *regarding* of the stone in hand – i.e., the stone was there before we picked it up and held it in our hand – therefore, our contemplation began sometime after the 'fact' of the stone. It follows that how we *regard* the stone is very much a part of how we cognitively organize the material objectivity of the stone. So, return to the problem, and rephrase: Is it true that I hold a stone in my hand or is the truth of the matter a cognitive *response* to the stone?

Asking such a question in this way implies the following: This thing called 'truth' seems in some way dependent on how our cognitive process works, while the material objectivity, in this particular case, the stone, as a *fact*, possesses a certain kind of organizing presence within the cognitive process. This suggests to us the generality that truth is found somewhere in the cognitive *process*, while the *certainty of fact* is found as a *principle* around which that cognitive process is organized. Truth is a process in our heads, while certainty of fact is the organizing principle central to that process. Where does this leave us?

Issues regarding the difference between truth and fact have considerable importance for all aspects of our personal, social, economic and political lives. The way in which questions concerning truth and fact are framed by professional philosophers can be located in any basic book on epistemology or truth[7] as they do certainly relate to 'true' knowledge. For us non-professionals, moving about in our daily and practical routines, the consequences of a distinction between truth and fact are, for the most part, as we have shown, hardly noticed. We might say that to be completely (and uncomfortably) on point, most of the actions of our lives *directly* concern truth just as they *indirectly* concern fact. Any closely observed legal proceedings will reveal that good criminal lawyers understand this distinction between truth and fact. With regard to nearly all our human actions we are mostly concerned with truth rather than fact. This is a temperamental statement, so to get at the disposition of this thing called truth we need to look beyond fact with a slightly different approach.

The phrase "this thing called truth" is used above to indicate that 'truth,' in a similar sense as 'fact,' has more of a thing-like sense to it than 'certainty,' which, curiously, has the more slippery feel of an abstraction. As discussed above, truth is clearly related to certainty, which is to say related to experience, but as opposed to certainty this thing-like *feel* to truth offers us something of a handle. Unlike certainty alone, or even fact, a 'truth' becomes an abstract almost real, almost as something we can grasp and *possess*. Truth has this quality of 'graspability' and 'possessability' because it overlaps both the cognitive camp and the material camp.[8] A truth, by the nature of certainty, can always be linked to something independent of our individual cognition, either as a *reflection* of material reality, a *manifestation* of relationships, or a *disclosure* of abstractions. Truth is not only a cognitive process but also overlaps the material objectivity that it cognitively organizes into "the thing called truth."

Truth having this thing-like feel to it also suggests something else – truth as property.[vii] In in this way it is possible to think of truth as something like a universal property,[9] a property *available* to all of humanity. If the Situation allows, it would seem that all humanity *can possess* truth. This in no way defines exactly what truth is, but makes it plain that whatever truth is, it is a thing which, by its nature, is a property which is (or should be) universally available. This distinguishes truth from certainty, which being rooted in ideology is rarely universal.

[vii] Property is merely a convenient descriptive noun that allows us to handle aspects of truth with expediency. It is not intended to imply anything necessarily physical or concrete about truth.

However, we need be somewhat circumspect about using the term 'universal property,' and especially note that 'universal' carries certain Situational (as opposed to ideological) elements which are sometimes at odds with its universal nature. A neutral statement such as "This is a stone," depends on a universal understanding of the object in your hand being a stone. But let us do a step-up into the less practical, but important Situational realm, and ask how we manage apparently innocuous and silly statements of the type "cats don't grow on trees." The only difference between a stone in the hand and cats-growing-on-trees is that you can handle one truth in the hand and the other truth only in the mind. Therein lays a pivotal point.

At first glance the claim concerning cats-growing-on-trees might seem utterly obvious and a true and factual statement under any circumstance. It is universally true that cats simply do not grow on trees! Is there anything biased or controversial about this claim? It would seem not. But as one influential philosopher (Wittgenstein) pointed out, we are certain that cats do not grow on trees only because we were taught this. [10] It became part of our experience solely through learning.

This exposes a hidden threat to the universality of even obvious truths. Unlike the stone in the hand, a statement about cats-growing-on-trees happens only in the mind. In another circumstance, if we were never taught, or otherwise learned, what was a cat or a tree, we could not possibly know how utterly obvious it is that cats don't grow on trees. This seems a silly suggestion and a waste of time, for in this reality where would such things as cats and trees not be learned from childhood? The answer is that if one were to look up the word 'cat' in a traditional Inuit diction-ary it could not be found, for the Intuit have no word for 'cat' in their traditional vocabulary. Situationally, cats were not part of the traditional Intuits life's experience, at least not before the coming of 'civilization' (a truly Situational expression). Of the long list of things the Inuit *value* in their reality, cats simply do not appear. As a consequence, without the word (much less the value) and the experience that generated the word, it would be absurd to convince an Inuit of the obvious truth that cats don't grow on trees. The traditional Inuit's external, or *objective* context, simply does not allow for the obviousness of the claim's truth value.

So, if there are some exceptions to the obvious truth that cats don't grow on trees, what are we to make of statements centered about such concepts as good and evil, human rights, racial inequality, democracy and social justice? It must be that 'truths' concerning these things, either simply or in great complexity, have been taught to us as well. This teaching, or the learning, that facilitates the internal organization of complex reality into truth, is Situational – that is, like the Inuit, our learning has integrated itself into our Situation. This raises basic social, cultural, and above all, historical connotations for our Situation. Namely, the manner in which we would learn to cognitively organize for truth in one time and place would be completely different that in another. It follows that the degree to which we value what we are taught will also vary not only with time and place, but also with the individual's Situation within that time and place. We might, for example, live in the same time and place as a physicist, but not be Situationally placed so as to understand the truth value of, say, dark matter. We cannot organize what we have not experienced. Truth derived from certainty might be universal, but experience is highly Situational.

It is not entirely accurate to simply conclude that what we are saying here is that truth is always relative. To say that truth is always relative implies that truth is only available under specific circumstances of time and place, and elsewhere it is unavailable. Obviously, this is not entirely correct. This also implies that truth is available only to a select few, and denied to others. This is a clever way to smuggle in elitist doctrine, but this assertion is just as wrong as the assertion about time and place. What *is* correct is that truth is universally possible while experience is not universally accessible. It is the *availability* of experience that is relative to the Situation. Once the notion of a cat is brought into the context of the Inuit, the Situation reconfigures so the truth of cats-don't-grow-on-trees acquires new meaning for the Inuit. The truth of the statement has not changed. It never changed. Only the Situation of the Inuit has changed. The truth was always there waiting to be revealed by a developing Situation. This reinforces the understanding that there is an internal or subjective condition to truth as well as an external or objective context.

What might hold a greater degree of relativity is the *value* of a truth, (value, like certainty, being rooted in an idea system) will clearly vary with the change of time and place. The Inuit, now understanding the truth of cats not growing on trees, might well dismiss it as a truth without any value and completely irrelevant, but the Inuit cannot dismiss the truth of the statement itself. For his part, Wittgenstein found the statement not just true, but also valuable and relevant. It seems that the value of a truth might be relative, but not the truth itself. We ought not dismiss values, but instead bear in mind the distinction between value and truth, which leads to the understanding that values are more relative to ideology than is truth.

In the learning of what makes up our Situation we have internalized some degree and type of truth regarding the social, economic and political entities which surround us. It follows that the degree to which we were taught such things as social justice produces change in the view of our context. For here, the basic certainty remains that truth, as internal organization of the external world found in experience, seems to have a functional relationship not so much with fact as experience, but with what we have been taught about context, or have otherwise learned about our context. Thus experience, as learning, becomes the processing factor for our Situation, and through the evolution of our Situation a new sense of truth is constantly evolving. In this way, learning as context is an integral part of the relationship between truth and our current reality. Like the Inuit, what we know and value about this world is based on a whole host of things that are tied to our Situation.

The truth of a thing clearly reflects something in context, but that 'something' is a complicated interplay of what we have learned, when we learned it, the depth and scope of the learning, the intention of that learning, and the material reality at which that learning is directed. This complexity is at the heart of the nature of the mirror that does the reflecting – our cognitive processes. If what we are taught, or have learned, has any bearing on truth, as it certainly seems to have, this casts a shadow over any notion of truth as some pure and objective reflection of reality uncovered in some one-to-one correspondence – a correspondence which, oddly, may hold better for certainty than for truth. Regardless of the thing-like quality to truth, it is most effective to consider truth as a *process* rather than an entity; truth as a process that turns on our ability to reason, which goes on to make *truth-as-process* the universal property, not truth itself.

Truth-as-process can give us the feeling that truth is something fluid, constantly shifting, dissolving and reforming. It is as if truth were a mercurial thing built on sand. At first blush this appears to be a disaster for truth and experience. At second glance, this is a disaster with a brighter flip-side. The Situation we can control to a much greater extent than we can control the context. Through control of the Situation we can change our relationship to truth, hopefully hold it more firmly in grasp. We have the choice to change our Situation through learning about our objective context, thus changing our relationship to truth. We can change our level of experience, which strongly implies that truth is a choice, or more accurately, that truth-as-process is a choice. The choice to change our Situation produces a unique *personal responsibility* we each have toward the flowing waters of truth. Along with the realization of truth (like certainty before it) as choice comes a special responsibility we have toward truth. We are responsible for our truth-as-process, and thus responsible for truth itself. Therefore, not just choice enters the realm of truth, but also responsibility. It is one of our responsibilities to choose the bringing of truth into the world.

Circumscribed by what we know, an involuntary linkage goes on between what we have learned to value and the way we have learned to observe. In that *involuntary* sense, there does exist a correspondence between what we have learned and how we assess truth. For example, is it true that the sun travels above the clouds and across the sky? Of course! The sun starts over there and moves across the sky. The sun moves, the earth remains still. It is as certain as the nose-on-your-face. As we choose to learn more about our context, our Situation changes, as does our relationship with truth. The certainty of truth in one Situation turns out to be only belief in another Situation, as ideology prescribes. As we choose our Situation, we choose certainty, and our truth. As our Situation evolves, today's certainty of truth may devolve into tomorrow's belief.

All-in-all, as our actions largely depends on our grasp of truth, and as experience develops, truth becomes an ever evolving process. Every fixed notion of the appropriateness of our actions must give way to an evolving process of the evaluation of truth. Truth is not fixed, but is part of our unfolding Situation. Riding on this shifting platform we bear a great deal of personal responsibility for not just our relationship with truth, but for the truth we choose to bring into the world. This seems a strange and awkward and daunting position – to say that our relationship to truth depends on our Situation, which within the strictures of time and place (maybe), is largely our choice, and our responsibility. But it is something with which we must reckon.

Ethics

Preliminary considerations of action and inaction

Quite simply, ethics is morality in action. Ethics a rule of behavior we choose in order that selected moral principles are put into practice. We might say, for the sake of facility, that ethics is the study of the rightness, or appropriateness in deed, while morality, as such, is the consideration of the 'goodness' at work behind the deed. So, roughly speaking, ethics is that branch of philosophy which studies what actions human beings ought to take, or not take, that will best lead to a morally 'good' outcome, and for what reasons ought they to take then, or not take them. Therefore, any inquiry that seeks to uncover the rational mechanisms behind the choices which individuals make, and how those choices affect them and the world around them, can loosely be said to provide a base level for ethical study. With some confidence, we can say at least this much.

Ignoring issues of morality, for the moment, this begs two preliminary questions concerning human action. These are two questions that have important – if not immediately cognizant – implications for understanding of ethics. (1) Do all actions possess an ethical dimension; that is, are all acts automatically moral in nature. (2) What is the ethical meaning of inaction? It will serve our purposes to look into these two preliminary questions in detail.

First, regarding the Situation we can take *nothing* for granted, no choice, no action. Our understanding of any sense of ethics depends almost entirely on our knowledge of familiar conditions in which many ethical questions arise. These familiar conditions can be deceptive. And the deceptions can be subtle. There are some actions that, ethically speaking, give every appearance of being of little or no moral significance. To illustrate: Whether you choose to knock on a door with your left hand or your right hand is (or at least appears to be) a trivial action, and of no possible ethical consequence. Yet let's consider that if you are a police officer – a rather obvious guardian and symbol of social morality – rather you knock on a certain door with your left or right hand (contingent upon which hand the policeman handles a firearm) may be of profound impact on the event and the consequences that follow. It should be obvious that the particular Situation offers up both ethical *and* moral ramifications. And consider another illustration: Sitting quietly and watching birds peck at food also appears morally piddling in the extreme, unless you happen to be Charles Darwin.[11] In this case neither the ethical or moral consequences bear immediate report, but the long range moral and ethical impact is staggering.

The police officer is a symbol of public and political morality and in many circumstances recognizes, by dint of training, that even what appears to be the most trivial of actions can have implications whose ethical dimension is yet to be revealed. The quiet observations by Darwin of the ordinary behavior of animals changed everything, forever, about our world. We have chosen two very different examples to demonstrate that it is not simply the circumstance of the action, but the Situation, (i.e., the interface of a unique context and a unique individual, each with their own special history) that spells the difference.

The point is that we cannot take for granted anything regarding morality as it unfolds in action. Nearly every action is Situational to one degree or another, which suggests that our ethical understanding of events depend a great deal on what we have experienced, and have come to *know,* as knowledge is a prime instigator of the Situation. This is not to say that there are no trivial episodes in life, but only that we cannot assume anything from the actions we see. We cannot depend on any automatic process to distinguish the mundane from the pivotal, nor can we assume the existence of some legal 'instinct' to recognize the right from the wrong choice. Our Situation is everything. If we are to assume anything, we must assume that every action possesses an ethical dimension.

Second, we must consider the implications of *inaction.* How many of us have decided against action, dusted off our hands and walked away from any decision to act. Are we allowed an ethical pass by this refusal to act? Have we dodged the consequences of action through inaction? This is Situational, just as action is, but in general the answer is no, inaction is never an escape from consequences, one of which is ethical.

Inaction is a voluntary act, or more accurately, a voluntary choice for action in the form of inaction. We often choose not to act in the face of possible alternatives. Something is none of our business, or we understand little or nothing of the issue, or we believe that only trouble will ensue from our involvement. So we *choose* not to act. Inaction is action as surely as is action. Not to act, no matter the reason, is a conscious decision to act and therefore a consciously made ethical choice. This does not necessarily make the choice for inaction wrong or in-appropriate, but we must recognize that in many cases not to act is a more deliberate choice than to take action and bears many consequences.

This steers us toward a powerful and often avoided point. In the face of ever present alternatives (and they are always present!) we can never avoid making decisions and taking action. We can never evade ethical choices and responsibility for those choices. We are uncomfortably ethical creatures, and by the circumstances of the Situation, we are creatures living ethical lives, for moral ends. We are doomed to live an ethical life. From this demand of our Being[12] in the world we cannot escape. We can only speculate on just how disheartening this conclusion must be for those who would wish to remain forever uninvolved. Non-involvement is not possible!

A. The Meaning of Rules (and the Meaning Behind Exceptions to Rules)

In a most general way, the rules that guide ethical action are established by one of the various systems of morality.[13] Right, wrong, to do or to not do, good, bad (or evil), correct, incorrect, better or worse, all these are just some of the moral catchwords that crop up to influence ethical choice and ethical actions. The words, and the ideas that lay behind them, underlie the ethical 'rules' by which we have come to believe that the choices for voluntary actions are made. The concepts that support these ethical 'rules,' concepts such as right or wrong, good or bad, which is to say morality, are endlessly wrangled over, teased, examined, poked and prodded, until there seems to be little left but a tangled haze through which we see the world in perennial shades of gray. This resulting shading often casts a pale over concomitant ethical rules in a way that makes them appear arcane and enigmatic. The pale ultimately offers morality a temporary and unstable feeling.

One source of these perplexities surrounding morality and ethics arise from our human ability to reason. Reason, fed by experience, grants us the power to be skeptical. [viii] As we mature we develop a skepticism concerning the nature of things. It is skeptical reasoning that leads us to question the fixed and universal nature of ethical rules and laws. If our context was steady and immutable, then questions of right and wrong, good or bad, will possess solid and sensible answers located within some predetermined scheme. If on the other hand, as we come to suspect that our human reality is less than fully foundationalized by meaning and purpose, suspicion is cast upon the rules, laws and the moral concepts that support what we must come to suspect are artificially induced by time and place. Defining moral issues and making solid ethical decisions become elusive and less tangible both for the individual and the society in which they find themselves.

Fed by reason, these ethical 'shades of gray' almost always make their appearance in the form of exceptions to the rules. A rule, a law, or the concept it rests upon, is often decided, argued to be universal, then quietly dissented on. [14] This is a common pattern. Dissent to rules appears to be ubiquitous and unavoidable, for on reflection it seems that there are no universal rules or standards of right and

---

[viii] To be skeptical is not the same as to be uncertain as detailed in an above section. To be skeptical follows more as the result of an educated rational process that leads to inconclusive results.

wrong that are truly absolute and applicable in all cases. As we will argue, there are no universal moral rules without exceptions. There is always the disturbing *but*.

Even while acknowledging the frustration it should be obvious that rules, principles and laws, especially those of a moral and societal nature, are desirable and necessary. This is so if for no other reason than that established rules grant to large groups of individuals the social and cultural stability necessary to carry on the practical affairs of every day life. More to our point in this project, it goes without saying that a solid feel for predictability and consistency is highly coveted by the individual in order to cope when considering our existential circumstance. Seemingly fixed and universal principles would stand as powerful rigging in that storm of existential unease that threatens to undermine our very sense of *what* and *why* we are. One way to cope with a sense of meaninglessness is to search out firm and changeless principles. This search is an obvious temptation.

As we have discussed previously, the want of a sound system of ideas supporting morality, and the ethics it drives, is an indirect expression of the need for an existential foundation. However, while the desire for foundational stability is a motivator behind the craving for fixed moral rules to guide ethical action, the desire is only loosely connected to issues surrounding the logical co-herence of morality and applied ethics in context. In other words, while the search for existential stability is one of the prime movers for developing moral rules, that desire for stability is not automatically related, in some one-to-one relationship, to the circumstantial expression of ethical action. There is a fuzzy but permanent disconnect between the moral foundation and the ethical application. Therefore, we can honestly claim that there is nothing ethically *wrong* with searching for universal moral rules and principles to guide our actions, while on the other hand acknowledging that universal morality exists only in idea-systems and as such do not universally apply to all concrete Situations. The development of rules and principles will grant us a passing sense of stability, but not a trustworthy ethics, that is, a guide to moral action. If we are going to develop a reliably consistent ethics we must start with something more dependable than a morality provoked by existential anxiety.

Properly viewed, morality and adjacent ethical rules do not happen in a vacuum. As argued above, their construction is driven by human anxiety and is therefore contextual. The only *directly* relevant questions which can arise concerning an ethical foundation are those questions concerning the social and practical motivation behind the development of the 'moral' rules. Moral rules arise in response to circumstance – actual, material circumstance nestled within an historical context – and they cannot be fully understood without acknowledging the circumstance and context that provokes their making. The study of moral context and response to moral context (i.e. Situationalism) is a most firm and appropriate venue for understanding ethics, *per se*. Situationalism is not the only venue, but given a foundationless humanity existing within a fluid context, it is the most practical setting to explore.

We can see that the underlying *motive* for any system of consistent morality is existentially launched. That is, morality, and the ethics that follow, is *motivated* by our primal circumstance, and therefore the procured nature of moral rules is *contextually* organized. Understanding context, circumstance and response, as well as the study of what are the intended and *unintended* consequences of rules – for there will always be unintended, negative by-products (sometimes called *blowback*) to moral principles in action (i.e., ethical action) – together with what are the exceptions to these rules and principles are the loftier goals of ethical study. We will touch lightly on them here and only in relation to the issues directly stirred by Situationalism.

If establishing universal rules are contextually confined, this would certainly go a long way toward answering their wide variety and their breath of exception. So let us ask whether or not it is possible for us to imagine an assumed universal rule for which there are no exceptions? Enter cannibalism, parental incest, polygamy, or infanticide (etc.)! These most strict of taboos, and others, are all widely assumed and accepted rules, and generally held to be universal among contemporary human societies. Yet, can we not imagine circumstances that would authentically warrant exceptions to these rules, even amongst westernized, so-called civilized people? Of course there are exceptions, and if exceptions can hobble the universality of rules against even these most forbidden of human activities, consider the serious damage exceptions can issue for rules about lying and stealing, or even killing another human. Are not all 'universal' rules are made pregnable by our ability to reason. There can be little doubt in our mind as to what is cannibalism, but have we not all, at one time or another, pondered the unfiltered and noncontextualized meaning of stealing, or even of homicide?

If it seems that there are exceptions to every rule might we then take it that there can be a rule that there are simply no fixed rules? This is awkward, as making a rule that there are no rules runs into a rather obvious paradox: If every rule has an exception then there is an exception to this rule as well. This irony logically makes the rule that every rule has an exception false. Maybe the most consistent way out of this catch-22 is to simply state categorically that there are no rules, not even a rule that there are no rules. There is only spontaneous assessment and judgment. At least such a statement – that there can exist a state of *no-rules* – would possess some sense of consistency. However, such a state also seems to force us into an uneasy acknowledgement of nihilism, not to mention a deep puzzlement over what kind of society could possibly exist without rules.

It might be that buried at the heart of the problem we will uncover a misaligned orientation in the way we face the ethical domain. That misalignment is the manner in which we are trying to meet ethical choices head on by insisting that moral rules can be made *a priori* rather than established as an integral and Situationalized piece of a continually evolving context. It is a mistake to think that our living context is anything other than a fluid process, with Situations perpetually evolving, blending the unique with the historic to form new and singular Situations which demand novel responses and all of this with no apparent beginning or end to the process. Thus, like sailing into the wind, we conceitedly attempt to force ethics to be a moral creature entirely of our own making rather than a dynamic process in which we must willingly participate. Rather than look at any ethical quandary from the standpoint of *how* are we thinking about the Situation, or what it is that we grasp about the *context* in which we are enmeshed, we tend to present an arcane ethical solution using an irrelevant moral blueprint. This is to say that misaligned ethical solutions may often be the result of a moral understanding of an entirely different circumstance, or it may have been transcendentally reasoned – allowing for the possibility that such reasoning is even genuine.

It seems more ethically appropriate to let us look at how we fit into the objective demands and necessities placed upon us by the Situation at-hand, together with the context which lends form and definition to the Situation. Such a 'look' would leave us as the responder to the ethical possibilities embedded within an evolving dynamic rather than promoter of moral rules established prior to the emergence of the Situation. In such an integrated approach the individual's reasoning ability becomes part of an unfolding Situational process rather than extraneous and quite possibly antagonistic to the process.

What we are saying is that in attempting to force the immediate Situation to conform to *a priori* moral standard we are inserting inappropriate perceptions into the process and thus losing any clear grasp of the context. This loss of context makes problematic any truly beneficial ethical reply to the Situation. Rather than use reason to influence appropriate replies to our fluid Situation, a Situation within an evolving socio-historical context, we use reason in a way that cuts us off from this evolution. In this way *a priori* ethical reasoning frequently provokes contextual incoherence. This incoherence all too often leads us to exist in an ethical contradiction with our Situation, contradictions most handily revealed by 'exceptions to the rule.' Capital punishment is an obvious example of this kind of contradiction and exception to the rule (against killing.)

We often see these contradictions and incoherencies revealed by those societal justifications which openly masquerade as universal ethical principles. A great many such principles, established *a priori*, are very often narrowly motivated prerogatives based largely on prevailing social relations and values within an immediate, existing historical context. These *a priori* establishments come to fit so discordantly with their immediate context that the ensuing contradictions engulf both the actors and the event. This is the most relevant explanation for many macro and micro calamities. Illustrations of this are in order.

The macro-Situation is the easier of the two to example. Many macro incongruities have been well defined and analyzed *ad nauseam*. To offer but one example, we well know the outcome of the discordant arrangement between the European landed nobility and the peasantry whose lives and production are at the command of this nobility. Eventually, the *ideological* support for the European feudal arrangement collapsed beneath the burden of incoherent *a priori* ethical principles. Such *a priori* ethical principles that propped up the feudal class structure arose as the moral ombudsman for laws of nature acting within a transcendental *ideology* of the 'will of God.' The concrete incoherence therein dictated circumstantial wealth for the few in a context of impoverishment for the many. In as much as a great many ideologies both derive and reveal their inconsistencies in contextual reality, the ensuing Situational contradictions overwhelmed the *a priori* moral justification as well as the ideological foundation for the feudal hierarchy. As the widening gulf between the producers and consumers directed the system's violent implosion, the moral system, along with its ethical and ideological deportment, collapsed along with it.

Less studied are the contradictions between the *a priori* ethic and the 'micro-contextual circumstance.' In the micro we will personalize a couple of Situations to illustrate the incoherencies and ensuing contradictions. For example, we can look at the case of the individual who chooses the 'individual right' to conspicuous consumption in a worldly context of dwindling resources; or the religious family that has the 'religious right' to refuses blood transfusions for their hemorrhaging child in the context of life saving medical science; or the businessman who demands the 'rights of property' and so joins a small consortium of industrialists that depress wages in the social context of a large but powerless producing class until finally there are no general population left who are able to afford what is produced. Incoherently, the *a priori* moral principles that compliment these self-destructive, contextual incoherencies persist long after the social pretext has been swallowed up in the contradictions.

Of course, many actions have these obvious connect-the-dots contradictions, and often the deciders in the events – either blinded by the justification or uncaring of it – are simply willing to accept these paradoxical disasters. However, far more often, most of the choices have unforeseen long-range inconsistencies that lead to remote and unanticipated consequences – unanticipated, as in the case of the Versailles Treaty's connection to the rise of the Nazi Party and the disaster that was World War II. Connecting the dots in these long-range cases is a difficult study and demands a required focus and a contextual analysis few are willing to undertake. It is far easier to shift the blame to a fickle fate, the alignment of the stars, or the 'damn fools' running the country, rather than recognize that detailed knowledge is vital to a successful investigation of the context. This balking at accepting personal responsibility for study and analysis also opens the door to the exceptions and contradictions

In either the case of a bald-faced willingness to accept the contradictions and consequences, or of being ignorant of them, the actor is likely to describe a *confrontation* with context as being the overriding consideration, and *a priori* choices thereby unavoidable. This makes the *a priori* principles not just agreeably digestible, but also facilitators of denial, allowing the actor and decider to resist the freedom inherent within the Situation – a freedom that is the *only* active element within all Situations that is authentically unavoidable.

B. Common Sense and *A Priori* ethics

We have also heard of a kind of reflexive understanding of events which purports to by-pass any kind of serious analysis, that is, an understanding that appears to evolve and reveal itself according to instinctual awareness of fluid circumstances. This apparently visceral, contextual 'grasping' of circumstance is often identified as "common sense." It is understandable that we frequently (and mistakenly) draw the conclusion that this common sense appraisal of the Situation is testimonial to an *a priori* moral sense hidden somewhere among our 'natural' gifts. We have been lead to understand that this common sense speaks to something more fundamental than the learned experience or practical wisdom garnered by such as a carpenter or a physicist; somehow the notion of common sense typically rests on a claim to something deeper than learned systems of response, something subconscious that resides in mechanisms innate to our nature as humans.

We might illustrate this commonplace proposal by asking a simple question: Do we give a child the availably to anesthesia prior to a painful but necessary operation? This is a highly instructive question, as clearly, and apparently instinctually, the common sense answer is 'yes.' Regardless of culture or social history, anesthesia is called for. We don't need pre-established rules, or even vast experience, as a means to establish the ethical end, for doesn't the vulnerability of the child demand that we protect it from pain? This is just common sense! This seems so obvious that it led the philosopher who brought up this particular example to the conclusion that such a common sense illustration represents clear evidence for the existence of *a priori* ethical knowledge as an objective fact.[15] Somehow, this philosopher argued, as a matter of "common sense," we know the ethics of this Situation prior to the evolution of the Situation, and we also know it without consulting pre-established rules.

Whether or not one calls this 'common sense' or not, the philosopher in question (Bambrough) does provide us with an excellent and relevant issue: are we, as a species, in possession of *a priori* instinctual ethical responses to certain conditions that supersede contextual moral analysis, and what is the possible impact of this 'instinctual knowledge' on our ethical choices? In other words, does the illustration of the child and anesthesia truly demonstrate that we as a species have some sort of natural grip on a moral foundation seen through a 'common sense' approach to ethics, and is an innately occurring 'common sense' paramount in establishing fixed moral relationships despite changing circumstance? If the answer is 'yes' then surely morality is a part of a human nature that overrides even changing conditions within an evolving context. Were the question rhetorical, this would be an extremely tempting conclusion.

Yet in spite of the above example of the child and the anesthesia, we have no clear scientific proof for any conclusion concerning 'instinctual knowledge.' And we very obviously *do not* have any strong instincts against causing or inflicting pain on other creatures, even our own fellows, even children. It is far more consistent to suggest that it is the particular Situation of the child and the anesthesia that predisposes our protective empathy. For example, consider that should the child need a leg amputated or die, no doubt the amputation would be done, with or without anesthesia. Inflicting pain, in this context, is clearly a secondary Situational consideration. Survival of the child is primary. In this case, the particular circumstance is pain, while the general context is survival as sensed through one of the many motifs of *vulnerability* – a concept that will play a most prominent part in later discussion.

None of the above is to claim that there is nothing we might safely call common sense, *should we wish to do so*. For example, it appears to be only 'common sense' that a 'past' existed prior to our having been flung into this reality, or that if one is reading the words on this page one possesses an organ for sight, etc., but does any of this really serve to establish a 'common sense' that translates into *a priori* knowledge concerning right and wrong, or good and evil? Such ethical considerations are truly qualitatively different positions with vastly different implications.

However, in spite of this, the suggestion of instinctual, common sense knowledge does allow us to explore a certain hidden topic of some considerable importance to this project. Question: Why do we have so many rules embedded in our cultural morals against harming others, but noticeably much fewer that require we help others? There are social rules (not to mention laws) against burning down your neighbor's house, but none that demand you come to the aid of the hapless individual and help put out a fire.[16] Why do we lean toward inaction rather than positive action? Can it be possible that we have a common sense instinct to *not* cause harm, but no common sense instinct to help? Based on the evidence offered by our social experience this would seem to be the case.

All cultures have more or less well defined rules prohibiting the causing of harm to others, but rules that would insist that we come to someone's aid are conspicuous by their absence. Existing social rules that might insist on helping others are far less structured, often spiritually orientated, deliberately vague, or simply non-existent altogether. Put another way, most cultures support existing legal rules (i.e. laws) that prohibit harm, but in the absence of cultural support for rules demanding positive aid to others the few legal support structures for such altruistic measures are weak and often conflicted.

This has not gone unnoticed, and there are some rather creative rationales for this prejudice against rendering aid,[17] but when carefully considered, there seems to be only one explanation with any sense of consistency (and this will have great meaning in the section to follow on 'What Can I Do?'). *To deliver genuine assistance to others we need to feel a special sense of empowerment generated by some unique knowledge or skills.* When stated so simply the idea seems not so profound, but consider that not knowing what to do, or not having the expertise to predict the consequence of our actions, renders us frozen, often in a state of high anxiety, and sometimes near panic. Acting in ignorance can bring unpredictable results, even grave harm. It is at moments like this that we feel an intense sense of vulnerability and are most likely to say, "Someone ought to do something about this." Based on a hasty Situational analysis of our incompetence, we make a conscious, and perhaps justified, decision toward inaction. Unless we are making a conscious decision to refuse to act because we wish a negative outcome to events, knowledge and expertise, (i.e., who and what we have chosen to become), seem to be the pivotal factors in the making of an ethical choice for action verses inaction. There seems to be a greater coherency offered by this existential explanation than some instinctual interpretation.

It is a cliché to say that 'knowledge is power,' yet once again we see that knowledge and experience enters in the equation to balance and influence our capacity and schemes for positive action. As we will see, the scope and nature of knowledge and experience will always find a central place in the debate over universal rules verses Situational ethics as they impact the individual. This idea of knowing, and knowledge of context as empowerment, will remain at the heart of all our ethical questions, Situational and otherwise.

As it seems to be where we are headed, let us look for just a moment into the question of living without pre-established maxims. Can we live without universal rules – or at least live without rules other than those which are of our own individual design? It makes no real, practical difference if we call this a 'common sense' approach or not, this is not so fantastic a question. It does allow us to openly speculate on the nature of the individual and a creative Situational ethics. Can we live with such a state as to deny that there are universal rules? What would be the core implication and significance of such a state for the individual and ethics? It might be that this would untangle us from a number of the inconsistencies, but what would be the look of such a state and the consequences? Words like 'lawless' and 'ethical anarchy' are too negatively charged to be of any real practical use in this analysis, and even 'common sense' is predisposed to awkward interpretation that can lead to a mishandling of most circumstances. 'Nihilism' is a better fit, if we can ignore the forbidding atmosphere of mayhem and terror it evokes. For now it is probably better not to use these words and concepts. Still, we can ask the question: What if there are no universal rules for the individual? That is, place the individual in a position to ignore social guidelines and define their own rules. What are the consequences? Is this an appropriate position for the individual to take and where does it leave us? It leaves us only with the individual and the Situation. Given this circumstance, how are we to come to the best possible determination of an ethical approach to such a shifting context? What would all this business of the context and Situation actually look like in practice? Rather than dream up imaginary scenarios, let us look at a few real world Situations.

C. *The Situation* Impacts

Just how might the Situation impact individual ethical choice? To probe this question we might draw illustrations from three main sources, i.e., from personal encounters, from social circumstance, and a cultural frame of reference. Given such a broad range of examples we should begin to get a general outline and common thread as to how the Situation impacts our choices, especially choices regarding what we tend to think of as right and wrong action.

Let's examine a personal example of ethical choice. For this we might take a rather detailed look at spousal abuse. There is no need to pass any kind of immediate judgment on this behavior to objectively observe that what is generally called spousal abuse is illegal in many societies in the world, but is given a wink and a pass in others. This conflict between legal and social attitudes by themselves raises the specter of contextualism, and together with the historical factors of class or religious ideology, one can see the difficulty of ferreting out a common and universal denominator. However, let us consider a context where spousal abuse is clearly both a social taboo *and* illegal. Where this is clear-cut we can see obvious *a priori* moral standards when analyzing the Situation. This allows us to contrast these with the personal ethical issues confronting the individual in a general personal context?

A realistic consideration immediately emerges from the idea of spousal battering. Should the battered spouse involve the legal authorities? This is far from an obvious and automatic process. There is a decision to be reached regarding reporting the battery, arrest and incarceration, all decisions having ethical dimensions. Clouding the choice is the great number of contextual factors involved in such a choice, *including* the fact that the battered spouse might be a male.[18] We should understand gender as at least one obvious factor in any decision to include civil agencies such as the police. This gender distinction creates a Situational issue that strongly influences both the ethical behavior of the battered and the batterer. As far more men are arrested for battering their wives or girlfriends than the other way around, it seems apropos for our project that spousal battery as influenced by gender can serve here to explicate the impact of the Situation.

For a male not to take legal action and refuse to punish the battering spouse (the wife or girlfriend) is an ethical choice to be made. It does not take reams of sociological and anthropological study to reveal the relevance of gender in this type of choice. Given the context of gender, we seem to immediately know why fewer men report being battered by women than do females when reporting being battered by males. Even if we call this common sense, it does not make it instinctual, which obviously it is not, yet still it presents a Situational dilemma.

So how might we resolve the ethics involved in this 'gender gap,' Situationally? What is the 'correct' ethical solution, Situationally? First, there is no solution which is absolute and beyond question. There appears to be no universal right or wrong answer. Some of us in the western world might tend to recoil from this statement in protest; spousal battery is illegal and punishment must be meted out. Gender is irrelevant! Nonetheless, in spite of this *legal* understanding, all of us can grasp the underlying reality behind the *ethical* equivocation. There appears to be a legal solution to handle gender, but no underlying correct ethical understanding, *unless* we sensitively draw the element of vulnerability from the mix. We have a clear sense that a woman appears more vulnerable to physical battery than a man, and less likely to survive the battery unscathed. Intellectually, we know that this is not necessarily the case. A woman can avail herself of weapons to redress the gender imbalance. There are numerous cases where spousal abuse has resulted in the death or maiming of male partners at the hands of a female. [19] Still, here lingers a residual undercurrent supporting the image of greater female vulnerability that steers us toward sympathizing with the woman as a victim of abuse rather than the man. [ix] Legally there exists a solution, an *a priori* rule, but ethically we realize that specific instances of spousal battery are contextualized. It

---

[ix] Recognizing this, we must also consider the factor of male 'humiliation' involved in bringing legal charges against a woman batter.

is this image of *vulnerability*, together with a serious grasp of some inherent *asymmetry* that offers considerable clarification as to the nature of the conflict between pre-established rules and the practical ethics of the Situation. There may be no clear cut ethical answer to certain features of spousal battery, but it does allow us to consider the cloudier aspects of the Situation

Let us imagine a case where both a male and a female cheated on their spouse. This is obviously not far-fetched and we can easily predict the emotional consequences upon discovery, together with the desire for some kind of retribution on the part of the aggrieved party. It would hardly shock anyone if battery took place. However, for a man to take physical action in the form of battery seems disproportional when measured against a woman exacting the same revenge regardless of the provocation. There is a certain kind of lopsidedness we can all recognize in this Situation. A lengthy analysis is not necessary to understand that different people would render different conclusions on the overall actions involved, conclusions largely based on knowledge of the context, or positioning toward the particular Situation. Even so, beyond this there is an even larger context found in the sense of transgressed proportionality, as it is reflected in a vulnerability that develops into a pressing desire to address the inequities rather than the crime. One of the parties is seen as more vulnerable than the other. Vulnerability is a serious underlying contextual factor which strongly influences any ethical understanding of the balance of right and wrong found in this type of Situation.

As the issue of vulnerability will increasingly enter our overall study of Situationism, a pause for a closer examination of this topic is warranted. One thing that we must note here is that vulnerability represents an aspect of symmetry that has a lasting impact on a carefully considered view of the Situation. Vulnerability obviously has a deeply emotional attachment to our sense of humanity, no doubt an attachment stemming from our own baseline instinct to survive. It is also possible that any imbalance might well be associated with some inherent neurological predilection toward symmetry. Experience tells us that imbalance, *per se*, appears to strongly rankle some un-defined hominal triggers. However, it needs to be noted that while both vulnerability and asymmetry seem to have a sense of universality, and given the freedom inherent in evolving Situations, either of these two human sensitivities, or both, can be consciously overridden as circumstances arise (e.g., legal circumstance).

Next, as a contrast to a personal encounter, let us look at a social circumstance. Consider an actual case. Some years ago, and despite the best efforts on the part of New York prosecutors, jurors refused to condemn Bernhard Goetz, the "Subway Vigilante," of violating serious New York felony laws which included attempted murder. [20] Even when awash in evidence of legal wrongdoing, the jury brought other Situational factors into play and refused to convict Goetz of gunning down the four juveniles who had accosted him on a subway platform. The jury seems to have made an ethical call that ran counter to the pre-established legal rules. The jurors had either personal knowledge, or a societal grasp, of the context that bound the Situation in which Goetz was the principal.[21] Even though the prosecutors were aware of this 'knowledge,' and had attempted as much as possible to cause the makeup of the jury to be representative of New York City demographics,[22] they could not overcome the contextual factors, which in the end Situationally overwhelmed the pre-established legal rules.

The prosecutors attempted to make the case that Goetz's actions were disproportional to the threat. The jurors clearly saw the disproportion, the imbalance, but saw it not in the way the prosecutors intended. The jurors simply had a larger ethical grasp of proportionality that superseded the pre-established rules of balance as codified by the state of New York. In the collective mind of the jury, Goetz acted *not* out of self-defense but out of a sense to right the imbalance of *vulnerability*. The jury made a gut call based on the instinct to survive. Correctly perceived or not, this instinct to survive manifested itself as a sense of the imbalance of vulnerability that all the members of the jury, to one degree or another, shared with Bernhard Goetz. It was this larger sense of vulnerability that presented the jury with the opportunity to make an ethical rather than a legal judgment.

Let us now look at a cultural scene that was chosen precisely because of its remoteness from our understanding. The anthropologist John Cook has observed that in certain Eskimo communities there exists a strange treatment of orphan boys.[23] The orphan boy is not fed by the community, but only has an opportunity to eat by going after food thrown to the dogs. This puts the boy in the midst of a fight for survival against hungry dogs. The villagers look on the contest for survival with apparent ethical indifference. We civilized observers are struck by the horror of the struggle, and the callousness of the community toward the boy's vulnerability. Then we learn that orphan boys, because of the unique cultural circumstance, go on to become the most fearless of hunters. The developed hunting prowess of these orphan boys comes to provide for not only their own family, but often, during harsh times, for the whole village. It would seem here that culture has conspired to cause the individual boy's personal vulnerability to be used to protect the larger vulnerability of the entire community. What we observers from the 'civilized world' have done is to project our ethical standards into a foreign Situation in such a way as to completely obscure the actual ethics as work.[24] The Situation has defined vulnerability in such a way as to allow ethical standards to arise to protect, not just the orphan boy, but the entire Eskimo community.

We might add, though it may seem somehow unnecessary, that there are many obviously 'positive' examples where vulnerability appears as the pivotal element in Situational decisions. We might illustrate this by offering the case of volunteering to donate an organ for transplant, or of the soldier dropping on an explosive to save the lives of fellow comrades-in-arms. In these types of cases the conscious ethical calculus swings on imbalance as it seeks to redress vulnerability. To right the imbalance of vulnerability is the most obvious calculation. While these examples have become clichés, they do represent extreme examples of positive influences inherent in the Situational address of vulnerability.

Others examples are more mixed, blending positive with the negative, and where vulnerability seems to come with a twin edge. We might suggest as examples of this the euthanasia espoused by such as Dr. Jack Kevorkian, or battlefield triage. In the case of euthanasia, vulnerability is the overriding concern, but it is so with an odd twist. The patient is vulnerable to life, with death being the redressing of imbalance. Battlefield triage leans more toward an ethical balancing act than vulnerability. Some, the most vulnerable, must be removed from the equation so that some others might balance the scales of life. These represent spontaneous ethical thinking and the most difficult of choices. However, they are not made by pre-existing rules, but on a Situational ad hoc basis with only vulnerability and imbalance to light the way.

In these and other cases, the issue of vulnerability and imbalance can be looked at from different points of view, and the decisions stemming from them argued from several positions. This is, however, somewhat beside the point concerning viewing vulnerability as the underlying universal principle in understanding the ethics of Situational decision making. We must also note that vulnerability hinges on proportion. This is a conceptual arrangement that can be presented as neither spiritual nor transcendental. Rather, it can be argued to draw its wiring from our evolutionary biology, that is, the survival instinct together with some sympathetic, inclination toward sym-metry and balance. We might call this sense of vul-nerability and imbalance the natural human scaffolding to Situational reasoning. The issues of vulnerability and redress of imbalance, as teased out of the circumstances outlined above, can be seen to extend to us a handle on spontaneous ethical thinking. We might even see it as a root of that seemingly instinctual 'common sense' understanding suggested by other philosophers – should we wish to do so. All this insists on elaboration.

D. Vulnerability as an ontological link

The above examples all display a concrete and temporal meaning of vulnerability as it can appear to us in everyday life. However, this does not explain the power of vulnerability to motivate us to altruistic thought and compassionate action, or why animals do not share the trait with us, despite the fact that animals certainly have an instinct to survive, just as we do. There must be something added to the human brew, something that refines, argues and augments our raw grasp of survival, a weighty element that tips the scale in favor of our coming to understand our actions in an ethical light. That 'something' that tips the scale is an *ontological* [x] sense of vulnerability. This is an intellectual sense of fascination and appreciation which we do not share with animals and is quite distinct from the unrefined instinct to survive. This is a vulnerability that flowers in the temporal setting, but has its genesis in our primal circumstance, that inaugural event in which we first locate ourselves and our human consciousness.

As discussed above, our basic ontology,[25] that is our fundamental sense of Being which emerges from our primal circumstance, and is devoid of the typical ethereal ra-

---

[x] Ontology, greatly simplified, refers to the study of issues surrounding the nature and meaning of existence (in this case human existence) as such.

tionales, [xi] causes us to look upon ourselves as without purpose and leaves us vulnerable in the face of our basic existence. These two senses of the vulnerable, the temporal, as derived from our survival instinct, and the existential, gathered from our puzzling and distressing ontology, are related and at times cross lines to co-mingle and charge each other with their presence. They can also be distinct, like when we might unexpectedly find ourselves temporally threatened, as when we might be stripped of our source of income and livelihood; this, as opposed to an existential threat, as when we come upon ourselves in an unexpected moment of angst in the face of our existence. To maintain the distinction we will call the primary source of this latter kind of fear and anxiety, *ontological vulnerability*. It is within this ontological vulnerability that the uniquely human seed of Situational ethics is found.

If we are to look upon this ontological vulnerability as a sense that is both human and universal, a sense that is distributed species wide, then we must consider it as either hardwired into our evolutionary biology or as a part of the ontology of our Being. Consider first, however, that evolutionary biology and the ontology of our Being are not necessarily exclusive. In fact the two systems may be complimentary or perhaps even symbiotic. It is entirely possible, even probable, that our ontology might be the perfect match up – the prefect contextual fit – for a human evolutionary biology favoring vulnerability. For the moment, let us consider that such a perspective would, at the very least, allow for a logical consistency, which, in

---

[xi] Usually, this implies religious rationales for existence, but other forms of spiritualism or mysticism can also be in play.

turn, would allow us to look on our ontology as a principle player in the development of any internal *predilection* toward ethical thinking. This is not to say that our ontology is a well-spring for some instinct underlying ethical reasoning. It is only a suggestion that our ontology *predisposes* our humanity toward an ethic that owes its existence to a special relationship with that unique sense of human vulnerability.

This sense of ontological vulnerability allows us a practical grip on both extraordinary and seemingly routine ethical assessments. As we have pointed out above, the underlying issue of vulnerability is one of the significant supporting struts for this thing we might want to call 'common sense.' Such ethical judgments, earmarked by vulnerability, often supercede or even run counter to a pre-established set of rules, as often does common sense. Not just the illustrations drafted above, but a little private thought will reveal that much of what we take to be right and wrong is based on our sense of *proportionality* as it engages with vulnerability, that is, an attempt to right some imbalance as it relates to the vulnerable. This provokes several pertinent questions. First, *why* do we feel this connection with a vulnerability that seems so influential with our ethical sense? Next, is this recognition and sense of vulnerability a species wide phenomenon, as it shows signs of being? And finally, if it is indeed species wide, then where precisely does it come from?

Since the mid 19th century philosophers have, with increasing consistency, challenged the ontological foundations of human existence. The rejection of the Godhead has been a primary focus for the busting up of any justification for human existence. [26] But, as we have discussed in previous sections, there have been other assaults on the grounding for our existence. Following these assaults we are left barren of any meaning or purpose for our existence. This nakedness has left us with a "fear and trembling and sickness unto death" (Kierkegaard). We can see this as pressing us into a cruel paradoxical dilemma: *our existence has made us vulnerable to our own existence* – we live in a subconscious dread of our own consciousness. This leads to feelings, again as discussed previously, of angst, or a free floating anxiety, and feelings of dismay and apprehension we cannot shake. If our sudden appearance on this plane of reality is merely a chance occurrence, without design, purpose or foundation, would we really be surprised at the arousal of vague feelings of vulnerability? To emerge from nothing, pass briefly into consciousness, aware always that there is no meaning to us other than what we ourselves assign through our own choices and actions, and pass quickly again back into nothing, is more than unsettling, it is *destabilizing*. The lack of stability engendered by such a suspicion of our ultimate, underlying meaninglessness would certainly present a vast and fertile field for unease and trepidation – but unease and trepidation over *what*, exactly? This is a vital question that insists on an answer. In so far as it is possible, we tend to suppress these feelings and get on with life, but where this 'fear' becomes conscious we are presented with a fork in the road. One leads to madness, the other to imagination.[xii]

[xii] We should always be aware of how intertwined are these two. The subject of imagination will take up some considerable room in the second half of this work.

If there is no point to our arrival here in this dimension of reality then whatever meaning is produced must be unhampered by previous principle or obligation. This frees us up. Thus unfettered, whatever intellectual constructs that design the principles and the meaning for our existence are *freely* produced *only* by us, and we are solely responsible for those constructed meanings. This '*freely* produced meaning' is a terrifying realization. It is also a realization that is very often hidden from us – by us. There is a desire to look away from this responsibility. There is a need to fabricate elaborate systems of ideas that serve as smoke and mirrors to hide from this understanding and from the pervasive mood of responsibility. The full grasping of this freedom is terrifying in its implications. It is only on deep reflection that the nature of this freedom becomes clear, as do the fearful implications of our responsibility for our actions within this freedom.

It is through this freedom that we also come into unavoidable contact with vulnerability. As we cannot escape our basic ontology, our primal circumstance, neither can we escape the vulnerability it entails. Our ontology is us, our freedom is us, and as such this freedom suddenly fills us with a distant but insistent sense of responsibility for *everything in our lives.* Through this sense of being responsible we can become overcome by an intense mood of vulnerability. Our vulnerability is inescapable because it is us. The unease and trepidation are not only over vulnerability, but also the fear of responsibility, and the fear of us.

As human ontology – as disclosed through freedom – is universal throughout our human species, the feeling of vulnerability it begets clearly looks to be a species wide phenomenon that joins us all. Human ontology links all episodes of vulnerability, such as the child facing a painful and dangerous operation, with Bernhard Goetz, with spousal abuse. All these events provoke an empathetic grasp of that encompassing sense of freedom and responsibility, *qua* vulnerability, the ontological bubble within which we all exist. However, a direct link between the ontology itself and the manifestations of that ontology are deeply hidden and not always quick to be revealed.

For example, ontological vulnerability can easily be seen to provoke a power response, or a selfish one, or an answer smacking of contempt and loathing, all those twisted sensations that seem devoid of any ethical consideration. As an illustration, witness the master and the slave, or the torturer and the tortured, or the camp guard and the inmate. As ontological vulnerability arouses fear and angst, it can just as easily trigger depression and rage rather than empathy. The camp guard's reaction to the vulnerability of the prisoner may well be to wall off any sensation of identification, refuse to look deeply into the utter happenstance of conscious life as reflected in the Situational vulnerability of the prisoner. Rather than experience the underlying meaninglessness as freedom, the guard might well act out the terror of freedom with the violence of a petulant child – the guard strikes out at the helpless prisoner. Though the origin is the same, the camp guard's reaction to vulnerability is the flip side of empathy. The guard lashes out against vulnerability by pummeling the vulnerable, raging in great haste to conquer impotency by punishing the impotent. Unfortunately for the camp guard, the torturer, the slave master, attacking the vulnerable does not erase the inherent vulnerability but only makes it rise up in self-judgment and self-condemnation, stoking the fear and angst, driving an endless cycle that the anger is not only powerless to control, but in fact feeds. This rejection of vulnerability is a rejection of our fundamental ontology and cannot help but lead to ugly and persistent symptoms – symptoms, as we might say, that are ontologically engendered and driven.

What we can say with confidence is that as we cannot outrun our ontology, we can never right the original imbalance. Like Sisyphus, rolling the great boulder of our existence up a hill, only to watch it tumble to the bottom again, we can only endlessly struggle to correct the imbalance inherent in our ontological vulnerability on this temporal plane. Our very existence fuels the struggle. History conspires and gives form to the intellectual struggle. Our ontology and our history shape our individual struggle which is the basis of our Situational ethic.

There is nothing automatic or instinctive in our relationship with vulnerability, or its certain connection with ethics. What we can say is that vulnerability is an element our species shares in common, but its expression is individually distinctive. This distinctive manifestation is an expression of the individual's historical and social positioning, a positioning that merely resides and is offered passionate impetus by our species wide ontological context. Another way to say this is to bring forward the claim that vulnerability represents an historical expression of our species brought on by our ontological condition, but is not a primary cause. We might say that vulnerability is our state of Being as resting on Nothing. This state of Being leads to a grave sense of brittleness. We exist in a state that is existentially vulnerable and whose expression is exhibited through historical precepts. Regarding vulnerability, we can say this with some certainty and imply little more – with certainty.

E. Situational Ethics

To sum up, we can say that when all is sorted out there appears to be two major elements that render Situationism a functionally dynamic ethical outlook.

First element: There is an animal wide predilection toward an underlying sense of vulnerability. This sense of vulnerability reveals itself most readily through the instinctual need to survive and be well. This is simply a part of us that we share with all animal species on this planet. What is different for we humans, as opposed to the rest of this earth's creatures, is an *ontological* vulnerability. This type of vulnerability has already been discussed at considerable length. Questions now arise concerning the ethical impact and individual importance of this ontological vulnerability.

This ontological vulnerability offers a *sympathetic predisposition* toward resolving imbalance inherent in temporal or material vulnerability. This predisposition readies itself through impending individual choice. We usually recognize the temporal imbalance with ease. The Nazi's invading the lowland countries, the plight of peoples in Darfur, being a couple of grosser examples. The asymmetry itself is quickly felt by our inherent inclination toward symmetry, but the recognition of vulnerability is also a part of us and at its deepest levels temporal imbalance is a reflection of our ontological vulnerability. We recognize the imbalance consciously, but even being marginally aware of the sympathetic predisposition to ontological vulnerability is quite an unconscious process; we identify this type of vulnerability through what seems to us, vaguely, as an instinct to protect, or a sense of guilt at the sight of the injustice of war, or lack of true fairness in living conditions found throughout the world.

To counter the vagueness, and be effective, this ontological sympathetic predisposition to the asymmetry of temporal vulnerability must be readied to take into account that the individual is armed only with historically conditioned possibilities regarding choice. These historical possibilities are the predetermined tools-at-hand derived from the system of ideas through which we grasp and interpret the world. When triggered by ontological vulnerability, these systems of ideas serve to organize the range of our choices of response upon witnessing imbalance. These responses are the making of judgments regarding the Situation, and help define conflict resolution in terms of right and wrong, or good and bad. These concepts lie at the heart of our notions of justice and injustice, though are never expressed in such a manner. Always, the judgments are activated by an overriding concern to redress imbalance regarding some real world vulnerability. The underlying ontological triggers are rarely acknowledged, even when and if they are marginally understood.

We must note, however, that all of this represents an ontological predisposition, not an automatic reflex. Our ontology is the impetus, the vitalization and concern for vulnerability, but not the tools to characterize and forge the *specific* choices between good and bad. These tools, and characterizations of good and bad, or right and wrong, are Situationalized. To rephrase: Always, the historical tools-at-hand are motivated and charged by the universal human ontology. The specific ranges of choices are part of the historically determined Situational-totality. For clarity, we need to flush out these claims.

At different stages of human developmental history, the individual is afforded different tools-at-hand, which is to say, a historically sculpted idea platform on which to stand and make assessments regarding the world around us. Underlying these systems of ideas is the motivation for a basic grasp of ethical conditions provided by the onto-logical foundation of our Being, the brute fact of our consciousness which arrives with our individual primal event. This raw state of consciousness grasps the basic understanding we all share for human vulnerability. This understanding is driven by a universal sense that we lack a purposeful foundation. This is the realization of our basic ontological dilemma. The specific details that tend to shape and shade the way we perceive and judge any view of temporal vulnerability form the ethical circumstances within which people find themselves acting as free agents. Different historical periods, and different cultural dispos-itions, color and bend our vision of ethical circumstances according to the idea-systems-at-hand. This leaves no room for universal absolutes in terms of right and wrong choices. Imbalance and vulnerability are confined by living experiences which are in great measure the consequence of choice, constrained and molded by particular historical conditions. The dialectical relationship promoting fluidity is apparent. However, the baseline of ontological vulnerability is always present. This baseline appears to be more directly related to our ontology than our evolutionary biology (though no doubt our primal circumstance *might* resolve into some type of sympathetic relationship with our evolution – this remains for future analysis). Right and Wrong, though vitalized and shaded by our universal human connection with ontological vulnerability, are nonetheless, historically conditioned and must be understood as individually Situational.

So, in practice, it would seem that whether we consciously wish to do so or not, we tend to view ethical issues through a lens of vulnerability – our *individualized* sense of vulnerability – peering from its ontological foundation through to its Situational expression. While the foundation can be considered universalized through a conscious humanity, the Situational expressions will vary greatly so that we must allow that vulnerability might appear irregular, or sensed differently, to a wide variety of individuals. Vulnerability in the human Situation is the key that unlocks the ethical dimension and allows us to sense an imbalance that aches to be righted. The historical context provides the tools-at-hand that enable us to search for a contextual resolution to the imbalance.

Second element: The second element that renders Situational ethics functionally dynamic is the power to act. First, if we are condemned to make choices, then these choices are conditioned by the nature of the historically conditioned tools-at-hand. Second, it follows that these tools-at-hand are the means by which we are empowered to facilitate choices. Therefore, these tools-at-hand are very much the basis of our power to act. They are the historically disposed conditions that allow us to see and adopt a range of choices.

These tools-at-hand, that is to say our antecedent conditions to action, are themselves actualized only through the knowledge and expertise we bring to the Situation. Consequently, the gathering of the tools-at-hand is our individual historical contribution to the Situation. The gathering of the tools is also our individual responsibility. Social historical conditions and individual responsibility play the ultimate governing roles in the evolution of any Situational action. The historical conditions cannot be changed, but the same cannot be said for individual, intellectual mastery. Our personal competence will change where we stand in relationship to the historical conditions and thereby alter those relationships. We are, consequently, responsible for our individual, rational proficiency and, albeit to a lesser extent, for future historical conditions. We make history, but on a scale concomitant of our intellectual capacity to act.

Our choices, unavoidable as they are, result in the changing of our Situation. This seems obvious. What is not so obvious is that by extension the boundaries of our knowledge represent limits on any changes possible to our Situation. If we possess no knowledge or expertise when confronted with the ethical sense of vulnerability, we can feel only helplessness and frustration with our inability to act in such a way as to right the imbalance and inequality. Our choices are narrowed as well as hidden by the lack of knowledge, a knowledge that is often historically or ideologically determined. Cynicism and anger are very often typical responses to these missing tools-at-hand. A dearth of adequate tools-at-hand is often the prime instigator of frustration fueled violence.

The desire to redress imbalance alone is not enough to make an ethic. As we said at the beginning of this section, ethics is about the choice for human action and its consequence. This rests on something more that an urge to right a wrong. There is a thought process behind the choices, a thought process that must consider the issue of the power to act. This means that both the urge and the power to act come only with an uncovering aroused by some special knowledge. Thus it is that the recognition of vulnerability, together with some special knowledge or expertise regarding that vulnerability, forms the basis of the power to act. These preconditions must come together with the special positioning one has to the context at hand, e.g., as were positioned the jurors in the Bernhard Goetz case.

We can see, from all that has been said, that the action dynamic which we bring to the context is our level of knowledge and expertise. This is the source of power to act, not the deep motivator, which is our ontology. It is through knowing that we can meaningfully affect and alter the Situation. To say 'knowing' is simplistic enough a word as to border on trite. Only 'knowing' is not raw, unprocessed experience, but a refinement of experience that become knowledge. Knowledge is what allows the Situation to develop a possible ethical resolution, a redress of vulnerability-balance. Knowledge is the rudder that steers Situational ethics. Without an incisive and profound knowing we are morally and ethically adrift.

What then, specifically, must we come to know? A complete answer to this question, in real terms, is found in the second portion of this project, 'What Can I Do.' For now, we are constrained to say only two things. First, that for our ethics to be effective our knowledge and expertise must draw its fire from our ontological grasp of the human Situation. And second it must be derived from a thorough and knowledgeable understanding of human freedom as it resides within the historical context. In other words, we must know what is *possible* in relationship to an ethical question or ethical goal and not necessarily what is *practical*. Very frequently practicality is presented as an ideological barrier, but what is practical is never a Situational one.

This is not as vague as it sounds. Practicality implies another *a priori* condition, another insurmountable law; to reason through such as practicality we must never lose sight of the precondition that right and wrong, or good and bad, are only contingent on the Situation. All Situations are unique. No law or rule can *a priori* supersede this understanding of Situational uniqueness. Through investigation of Situational uniqueness we are free to present flexible evaluations of right and wrong rather than accept the conventional (i.e., practical) solutions offered by some autocratic covenant.

Totally ignoring Situational uniqueness often results in catastrophic blunders. Examples of this failure to recognize Situational uniqueness might be illustrated by events as divergent as the Battle of the Little Big Horn to the Balfour Declaration of 1917. This Situational uniqueness must be carefully thought through and must be consistent through our grasp of human ontology as it rises in sync with our intrinsic need for balance and harmony. Of course, this 'grasp' must be compatible with historical context and conditions. As previously stated, a more complete response to this will is the quest of the second part of this project, 'What Can I Do.'

F. Choice, Responsibility and Connectedness

There are three basic features of our reality (as derived from our ontology) that all the above examples served to emphasize. (1) That we choose; (2) that by choosing we are responsible for 'everything;' and (3) that through responsibility our species is universally connected. At this point we are familiar with the first feature. The second suggestion comes across as a little weird and begs careful scrutiny. The third, while emerging from the second, also wants a careful parsing so it cannot be dismissed.

First feature. Our very existence assumes choice. Indeed this feature has been the primary and general underlying principle for this entire work. The very fact that we exist in the way we do makes choosing impossible to avoid. Our choosing may not be well informed or even informed at all, but choosing is nonetheless unavoidable. Enough has already been said on this aspect of our reality that we will not pursue it further here.

Second feature – and it should come as no surprise, given all that has already been discussed in this project – that since choice is impossible to avoid, so is personal responsibility impossible to avoid. The next step is to track down the precise nature of this responsibility. We must decide on the reach of personal responsibility, and determine exactly what it entails.

It is our human fate to feel some sense of guilt in making even prosaic choices, (e.g., I shouldn't have spent the money on this trifle; I shouldn't have spanked my child; I shouldn't have called in sick at work). A few find themselves in Situations fated to be not so prosaic, and where the guilt can hang ominously ('captains of industry,' and 'world leaders,' are categories that come to mind). As we are responsible for everything that we do, this means that we ultimately stand rooted in some morass of guilt for having arrived, for merely living. By its nature this must be a universally shared sense of guilt and responsibility. A digression, but these statements need elaboration.

Responsibility is more than a simple and uncomfortable by-product of the demand to choose. It is a great source of a permanent, existential condition of anguish. If the nature of our existence forces choice upon us, then the nature of our existence produces for us a ubiquitous sense of responsibility. After a fashion, this breeds in us an amorphous mood of guilt by (and for) our own existence. In a way, one might view this guilt for existence as the 'original sin.' Of course, such a notion of 'original sin' is a collateral consideration, and as far as this project is concerned, of secondary interest only. However, as much of great literature suggests a consistent, if latent burden of guilt (e.g., *Hamlet, The Grand Inquisitor, The Stranger*, etc.) we must not be so cavalier as to dismiss such an elementary theme piercing the human experience.

On top of this existential guilt we are doomed to make choices and feel responsible. Recognize that it is completely impossible to avoid feeling responsible, for we are responsible for every action we take. Even if we elect to not choose, we have not evaded ethical responsibility. 'Not to choose' is clearly a choice, and no matter what the reason we are responsible for the consequences that follow our having not chosen.

We choose a thousand times a day and each choice ushers in the weight of responsibility for having re-structured our living context, and therefore we are re-sponsible for continually updating the Situation in which we find ourselves. This is a way of saying that through our choices we are responsible for reconstructing our individuality. However, this is not all that our individual choices reconstruct. Our individual choices develop both our individual Situations *and* the context in which all humanity works out the array of future alternatives from which to choose. This last sentence is a bit jarring and the balance of this section is devoted to its analysis.

From the moment that we are aware of another separate reality, a reality where we are presented with alternatives, we begin the process of choosing the truths we must live with and upon; unavoidably, we accept the responsibility for those chosen truths. At first glance there seems a ridiculous aspect to this claim. How, for example, can we hold children responsible for their choices, which, if choices are made by them at all, are most often made without guidance, supervision and out of an ignorance of alternatives? To fully appreciate this 'ridiculous aspect' it is critical to note that the optimum phrase offered is 'ignorance of alternatives,' and not 'responsibility.'

This brings clarification to the idea that it is impossible for adults to *choose* ignorance. From a certain point in our maturing experience we are aware that we exist within context, and as we grow and are educated that contextual realization continues to expand and gain depth. From the budding of this awareness comes the realization that all Situational alternatives existing within contextual systems are at the root of the demand to choose. This is a rather long winded way of stating something rather obvious. Even if adults are not certain as to the nature of the alternatives, they are at least aware that somewhere in their reality alternatives are in play. Small children, on the other hand, do not abstract themselves as a separate living thing within a context and are therefore unaware of the alternatives around them. It can be said that children, in the absence of awareness of context, are truly ignorant of alternatives. This is inherent to the nature of childhood. For the child, as contextual realization has yet to come upon it, alternatives have not entered into the realm of thought.

A child who is not forewarned as to the consequences and therefore sticks a hair pin into a wall socket to suffer a bad shock can be said to be responsible for that choice in only the loosest (and perhaps meaningless) sense of the word. However, for the child to take the same action again, and suffer the same consequence, the child can be said to be Situationally responsible for the choice in the narrower sense because knowledge has altered the child's Situation. The child has developed some meaningful appreciation for contextual awareness along with alternative choices in behavior.

Of course, the absence of alternatives can also be a practical fact. Contextual conditions that clearly exist in some circumstances, can be absent in others. The above illustration of the butcher of Wittenberg in 1637 can be used to point out that it was not possible to make a choice of traveling from Wittenberg to Moscow in four hours as opposed to taking many days of travel because the context in which the butcher lives denies such alternatives; the butcher can take a carriage to Moscow, or even a fast horse, but airplanes are denied as an alternative choice. This seems an obvious, practical fact.

Another question: Is it possible to consciously *choose* ignorance and thereby dodge responsibility? We have often heard the old saw that 'ignorance is no excuse.' This is typically intended to mean that ignorance of the law is no excuse for criminal behavior. However, this old saw applies in general for the making of poor choices. Why? The answer is that we are aware of our context, and aware in more ways than we might care to admit. To admit contextual awareness is to admit of the *possibility* of existing alternatives. The acknowledgement of *possible alternatives* opens the door to personal responsibility. It becomes our responsibility to seek out these alternatives and offer them the best analysis of which we are capable. We may choose to feint ignorance, or to deny reality, or to actively choose to remain as much in the dark as possible, but none of us can completely avoid awareness of our context, which is to say the awareness of the possible existence of alternatives. We might be ignorant of the alternatives, but not of their possible existence. Refusing to explore the possibility of alternative choices is a choice in itself and therefore ignorance is a choice, and one that is anchored in personal responsibility. Exploring and learning are therefore two other uncomfortable obligations we cannot dodge.

Perhaps we can simply claim that we are merely too lazy to delve deeply into the contextual matters surrounding us, but far more often our laziness is a disguise for increased fear of the consequences brought about by knowledge; fear makes us desirous of ignorance. The pursuit of knowledge and expertise is time consuming and often tedious. To be sure the pretense of ignorance, or some outright denial of material reality, is easier. Nonetheless to remain in utter denial – if such a state is even possible – would be a choice that is consciously made. Therefore, any choice that ensues from ignorance is still one for which we are responsible. Contrast this with the action of a very young child. To not grasp the living context is to be authentically ignorant of the existence of alternatives. This means that the young child, Situationally, has literally no alternative choices offered by context and therefore the child bears no authentic responsibility. To exist in this world, and be unaware of the possibility of alternatives, would be a Situational extension that is authentic only so long as there is no realization of a contextual reality. Thus, excepting for the schizophrenic, a lack of this realization disappears at a very, very early age. We, the sane who are aware of context, might lack the resoluteness or courage to delve into these alternatives, but this is a different condition than simple awareness of the existence of alternatives, which we cannot avoid.

Are we always in a position to make free choices? Are there not conditions where we can justifiably say "I had no choice!" Consider the slave who is whipped into giving submission. Is the submission a voluntary choice? Is it truly realistic to claim that the slave is in a position to change the condition of slavery? And what of the tortured partisan who gives up the names and locations of fellow partisans to the torturer? Can we authentically claim that this choice to turn on one's comrades is freely made?

While we may never face such extreme Situations as does the slave or the tortured partisan, we must note that such Situations have existed and are therefore not mere thought experiments, or figments of a philosopher's imagination. We must take these questions seriously for they greatly impact the ethics of the Situation. Even today harsh labor conditions – even slavery – and inhuman treatment of prisoners continue to exist. How do we respond to the claim that there was no choice for the action of the slave or the victim of torture? As difficult as it may be to process, we must conclude that there remains always alternatives and therefore always a choice. It might be possible for the slave to run away or to go after Master with murderous design.[xiii] The victim of torture can plot and devise ways to stop the torture by bringing about an end to the misery through quitting life.[xiv] The alternatives might run from the unsavory to the extraordinary, but again the

---

[xiii] From Spartacus to Nat Turner, the examples abound. It might also be noted, in passing, that at the end of their lives, Spartacus and Turner died, by their choices, as free men.
[xiv] The death of Mahnaz Tehrani, 22, in June of 2009 serves as recent example; for details see http://iranfocus.com/en/special-wire/young-woman-commits-suicide-in-iran-prison-after-torture-17910.html

key word is 'alternatives' and not 'extraordinary.' To any specific Situation there always exist alternatives that lie within the context in which that Situation is anchored. They might be as harsh and as extreme as the Situation, but they do exist. Unfortunately, we must also admit that many of us would lack the courage to choose the offered alternatives, and this is nothing to be overly ashamed of. The alternative may represent the most disagreeable choices we might ever face and indeed we might break down in the face of these alternatives. But again the key word hangs: *Alternatives*.

The bottom line, as we read these words, is that we know very few of us will ever face such extreme circumstances as slavery or torture. Yet, even so, we all recognize that a good many of our choices are difficult, even if not so difficult as these examples. One can come up with any number of less extreme Situations where the choice can be said to be coerced – for example, the journalist who must give up the source for a story or suffer jail, or the pacifist who, facing military induction, flees to another country – but again the key word here is 'choice' and not 'coerced,' and therefore the choice is freely given; the journalist can certainly go to jail, as many of that profession have shown such courage and have accepted the responsibility to do, and the pacifist can quit one country for another.

On the subject of personal responsibility, we must state first that responsibility results from individual choices. If this project has meant anything at all, it has demonstrated that all our choices are ours and ours alone. In the last analysis, no choices we made were truly coerced and none were made by others. It follows that those who are the immediate intimates of the chosen actions have personal responsibility for those choices and their effect. This should be obvious and beyond any necessity to analyze. For lucid adults there is no excuse for not knowing that striking someone, shooting someone, or participating in universal military conscription does not entail personal responsibility and also concomitant degrees of social consequences.

What of more common predicaments? What of those circumstances, while unusual, that we might more routinely encounter; the unaccustomed circumstances that are found in our experience, yet are not so extraordinary? In our employment we undoubtedly encounter choices that affect others. In these circumstances we encounter rules and protocol that define the job. Do we blindly follow rules and protocol and evict someone from their home, charge exactly the same price to all, hire one person over another, pass one student's essay and fail another, etc? Do we attempt to evade responsibility by obedience to the rules? Or do we examine each Situation independent of rules and make a choice that is not bound to rules but drafted from an awareness of imbalance in relationship to human vulnerability? Both ways, it is a choice and as individuals we are solely and utterly responsible.

Within each of these Situational circumstances there exist at least two universal consequences for the choices that were made. These universal consequences affect not only us, but the world around us. First, as we choose Situationally we reveal to all around us a world of contingencies. As we choose, we direct attention to the power found in the mere existence of contingent alternatives. And second, in uncovering contingencies we also alter the context in which the contingences are made available to those in the world around us. This points out that a changing context multiplies contingencies and their availability. It changes everything. Both of these consequences bring about an impact on our conscious awareness that is of some considerable magnitude.

Third feature. Derived from our ontology there exists – and in great part rooted in the elements of choice and responsibility – a thing which we might, for the sake of facility, call *universal connectedness*. Through our choices we connect with the rest of our species. Such a connection has already been hinted at, at least as an abstraction. There is a more practical and concrete relationship between choice and connection, one that greatly broadens our responsibility, and also universally deepens our sense of guilt. This last claim is sweeping and needs to be unpacked.

There arise living extensions of the choosing that are the results of our having chosen. As individuals, we are not like atoms spinning wildly off into space. We individuals can only make sense and give meaning to our lives within a social network. For better or worse we are joined at the social hip, corralled with the rest of our species, both historically and presently. We are not one, but many, locked in an embrace of choices. When we choose, we choose socially and historically. The living results of our social choices tend to hide in the impersonal, practical details of life. The grasping of these practical consequences of our choices in its fullness demands seeing the forest in spite of the trees. All too often our personal world of choices conceals an inescapable universality of connectedness inherent in nearly all of our choices. In a meaningful, practical sense, this connectedness operates in a nearly infinite variety of ways, as the following examples will demonstrate.

First, we might look at a type of heinous activity. What of the factory worker that rolls the metal for the cans packed with Zyklon B bound for the Nazi death camps? Although it is difficult to decide, it is a legitimate question to ask just how responsible can we hold this factory worker for the deaths of countless thousands of innocents? We suspect, correctly, that there exists some level of personal responsibility. It is pinpointing the precise level of personal responsibility that is elusive, but surely it is there.

However, beyond a personal sense of responsibility, the example illustrates that we are all, as we have said, joined at the hip, which allows all those existing alongside the factory worker (e.g., family members, friends, neighbors, etc.) to be lifted to some level of collective measure of responsibility – for the Zyklon B, for the death camps, even for the rise of the Nazi party. We must add, however, that the knowledge of what was the final use for the rolled metal does increase the level of responsibility for this factor worker. But, the worker will complain, he has to have a job to eat and pay rent, he has to work to live. But is this entirely correct? Think! There is always a choice.

There are many more commonplace illustrations that also demonstrate the social web that connects us all. For example, it has become something of a cliché to point out that in the purchasing of a certain article of clothing we, in the affluent world, connect and offer economic support (along with the implied ethical approval) of overtly exploitive labor practices, usually in some distant Third World country, where harsh working conditions are out-of-sight-out-of-mind. With many of these choices, we can shutter our consciousness with distractions and go on with our every day living. The shuttering has little effect, as our choices in such cases are part of our living context, and are not at all passive choices. Through such choosing we connect with others – in this case the victims of offensive exploitation and their masters – in both ethical and real terms. These kinds of choices have ethical meaning to be sure, but there are also real consequences for us and others in our immediate Situation. In choosing to honor exploitive labor practices, the blowback might come in the form of outsourcing domestic jobs, perhaps your job. This is one type of real connection that is at the heart of our project.

It should also be affirmed that not all connections are negative. When we choose to take on extra responsibility for others, the elderly, the sick, the indigent, or abused children, the connection is obvious. Through these choices we begat a rippling atmosphere of caring that goes far beyond the immediate connection. The same can be said for selecting lifestyles, from fashion to enter-tainment to scholarly research. These choices not only press society's resources in a certain direction, but also develop a universal state of mind for an acceptance of a way of life. When we see vulnerability being unleashed, as when a when a person who is handicapped, has a regional dialect, or who hold unfamiliar but harmless ideas, is made the butt of jokes and we let it stand unaddressed, we tip the imbalance further for the whole society. As individuals we choose all for all.

Take as another example, a common Situation in western style democracies, a Situation that connects all in an unforeseen way. Suppose we step into a voting booth and vote for the opposition party, that is, vote *against* the existing regime in power. The unannounced is that we actually offer support for the existing political structure and all that structure might entail for the people touched by it. This apparently convoluted process is actualized through the act of voting itself. This act of voting reifies and legitimizes the 'democratic' system that is the historical, cultural, and legal pillars supporting the existing social structure. Thus, the simple act of voting frequently has consequences world wide, connecting with people and conditions far beyond the imaginings of the individual voter. Given this understanding, all those who *do not vote* on Election Day are the only ones actually voting against the regime in power. Through the conscious choice of non-voting, the non-participants reject the system that legitimizes the existing regime and all that legitimizing might imply. These people vote with their feet, as it is sometimes said. They choose for us all by refusing to 'choose.'

Thinking practically, 'voting with one's feet' does not overturn the existing order, nor does it reverse the un-iversal ethical system that sustains the existing order. However, when masses of citizens demonstrate negative participation this does work to connect with and strengthen the mass social consciousness. The choice of non-voting does connect and affect general awareness of the system's viability – and vulnerability – for all persons living under that political system. Through the choice of non-voting, the system begins to look less secure to everyone touched by that system. Viability is reduced through lack of participation in the support network. Thus by the choice made by a few non-participating members of the social order, the general world view of the many is tweaked and a new contingency is revealed.

Economics and political actions are not the only source of connectedness. Organ donation, which is commonly found on an automobile driver's license, has obvious universal consequences. This demonstrates the universal impact of choosing positively for others. It was not always so. The universality of such a choice was once totally individual. But when enough individuals independently made the choice to donate organs the choice crept into the public consciousness. Such positive possibilities were not only placed in our minds by the first to choose these types of selfless donation, they were, again by the process of choice, placed in the universal ethical community. Because of these individual choices, community wide ethical choices on organ donation are now an integral part of universal, ethical thinking. A few individuals made the choice for all.

More difficult choices regarding the various types of triage – and not just the medical type – represent mixed degrees of positive and disagreeable, perhaps negative choices. Triage types of choices represent the most studied types. They are the common grist of drama and literature and frequently involve only a handful to a few hundred people. Who gets prosecuted for a crime and who goes free, who is treated for a disease and who dies from it, who wins a coveted social position and who loses? All of these individual decisions greatly affect economic, class and political structures in a given social order, which in turn can touch millions. To make triages choices we must hopefully examine a great amount of information and do serious analysis on the impact of vulnerability. All this energy and work pays off for the entire social atmospheres of ethical choices.

As a slightly more esoteric example of universal connectedness, one might suggest that through our choice of information medium (e.g. whether you buy a newspaper or magazine, to tune into a particular radio station or view a television channel), you offer by this act not only an acceptance of a particular way in which your information is managed, but also choose for all of us the manner in which the our context is reified and reflected back at us. Such choices can represent both positive and negative universal choices. These choices, and the responsibility they entail, must also be carefully weighted and analyzed.[27]

The dilemma of choice and responsibility is increased by our technological world where the conscious choices we make constantly put our context in danger of *disintegration*. This technological impact is a very real and practical problem. For example, our choice of information flow, mentioned above, is not merely a selection of a political slant to 'news' content. It is also the manner in which we actually lose our living context to a medium that disrupts cohesiveness. In a very new and real way, technology threatens us with de-contextualization, which in turn threatens coherent, Situational development. This de-contextualization also threatens ethical systems. What do we mean by these strange claims?

G. De-contextualization and Connectedness
1. De-contextualization

The reality in which humans live, and have lived, is laden with experience. It is everywhere raw and unfiltered. The way in which this raw experience is processed gives birth to our Situational growth within a personal enveloping contextual awareness. The overall growth of this contextual development affects the perception of alternatives that come to be the choosing of our Situation. The young child who sticks a pin in an electrical outlet and is shocked has raw experience refined. This allows the child to make a more informed choice the next time. The child's Situational position has matured and developed. As this Situation develops, so has the child's overall context been reconfigured in a way that allows for a better vision of alternatives. How raw experience gets handled is critical to the contextualization in which our Situation is individually chosen.

In our contemporary, technological environment we receive very little raw experience. To a certain extent a lack of direct, raw experience was always been the way. It is difficult to imagine our humankind absorbing virgin experience, unfiltered by others, lacking any kind of interpreted message. Historically, we would have received our information from storytellers, from decrees, or from friends, family and travelers. This would have been part of the social context in which people have always lived, a part of the ideological atmosphere which nurtures development.

However, while the message was not undigested raw experience, neither was it so often deliberately manipulated for the benefit of individuals we do not know, or in the employ of a deliberate doctrinaire world view operating in the service of others. In stating this, we acknowledge the meaning of doctrine as being the real world expression of the canny and shadowy undercurrents of ideology; ideology being the parent of doctrine, and not just political doctrine.

In today's world our experience is carefully fragmented and intentionally rearranged and orchestrated. We should not think of this as necessarily a conscious conspiracy. Those involved in the re-composition of experience may only be unconscious doctrinaire marionettes trapped within the bounds of a historically fitted ideology. Yet, even though the design of the re-arrangement may be unintentional, being completely oblivious to the self-serving nature of the doctrine is difficult to conceive. We might example such a circumstance by looking at the thousand odd years of the medieval period in Europe. During this period the common world view was dominated by a God-centered ideology that produced a church doctrine largely acting in the service of the feudal hierarchy. To the crafty political analyst, the subtle (and sometimes not so subtle), use of ideology in this circumstance – transposed as doctrine – was (and is) patently obvious.[28]

In the modern world the effect of doctrine may be intended to attract commercial sponsors, and in so doing, modify the News in such a way as to offer little offence to the commercial sector of the economy. Of course, this modification has significantly brought information flow into line with an idea-system that supports the economic sector and shields it from direct criticism. The individuals involved in this orchestration may not even be aware of this, a least not in these terms. Rather than thinking of this as a conspiracy of individuals, it serves a greater objectivity to consider this a conspiracy of the historical circumstance that developed the ideology in which the individuals are immersed.

But whatever the case, our social experience in all forms – political, cultural, social, etc. – arrive in the form of snips, or managed slices, of both the fluid and the concrete. Call these managed snippets *info-bites*. In bits and pieces, we are told by numerous and unknown others what to see and how to see it. Not only does this management of info-bites interfere with the development of the Situation, but it also completely disrupts the focus which is so vital to the integration of experience with contextual awareness. Thus our Situational experience becomes increasingly incoherent and *de-contextualized*. Again, let us remind ourselves that such an effort may not be of conscious intent. Idea-systems work to insure that the way we perceive and handle experience appears intellectually satisfying and even personally copacetic.

Obviously, this fragmenting of experience greatly impacts the way in which we organize the perception of our context. What is more, as Situational analysis issues from within context any resulting attempt at analysis will reflect this lack of a coherency, though this is often not immediately apparent. We might say that through the employment of fragmented experience the trees (the Situation) are removed from the forest (context) rendering the forest (context) invisible, so that the Situation becomes at best contextually rootless (unstable and uncertain). We cannot fully develop our Situation around info-bites. To fully realize our individual Situation, we must abandon info-bites and search for different, holistic ways to refine experience into knowledge.

We can also describe this state of affairs by saying that as our context *de-reifies*. That is, our context disappears from our consciousness as something concrete and whole. Our context becomes transmuted and fluid, augmenting insecurity and a mistrust of what we experience. Through the technology of info-bites we see the whole of humanity as random and disconnected images, and the 'disconnect' comes upon us unannounced, and ironically, the disconnect worms itself into a contextual part of our Situational development. As a consequent, any capacity to Situationally analyze becomes increasingly unstable and worse, impractical, and will fragment even our raw experiences through a lack of integrated cohesiveness.

For want of a better term we often think of these disconnected info-bites as some form of *entertainment*, but the reality here is far more insidious. The promoted lack of coherency increases our feelings of isolation and aloneness. This develops a frame of disconnectedness which, as our sense of responsibility fragments, greatly increases our feelings of free floating anxiety and guilt. Along with the anxiety, de-contextualization also establishes an intellectual parochialism that stands in contradiction to universal connectedness. The total effect of de-contextualization is that it fosters a yearning for external ethical principals and mandates. For the sake of stability and completeness we can come to seek out rules and laws made by others, and never mind that these rules are most often constructed for self-serving purposes that violate our own best interests. De-contextualization hampers any clear vision of this.

With education we can choose the political and social slant on information that offers the greatest coherent input, but the paradox of a fluid, yet de-contextualized medium is far more difficult to grasp, and to successfully manage through choice. Such management and choices demand that we garner the ability to stand outside our context to fully comprehend the de-contextualization. The choosing of such a path would require an effort and knowledge of the available sources of information beyond any typical scope. This is not impossible, yet it needs to be stressed that any such engagement with our context is a demanding and time consuming process.

The first acknowledgement of any such demanding engagement is to be aware of the historically driven de-contextualization of our Situation. This is just a way of saying that we must be aware of the changing nature of our context and become increasingly aware of the absolute existence of alternatives. The main threat here is that due to de-contextualization we may not recognize the alternatives as they will also arrive in bits and pieces. The alternatives might well appear as random and disconnected info-bites. To overcome this disadvantage brought on by contemporary life, it is we who must bring cohesiveness back into the dislocation. We will accomplish this through the uniquely human feature of *imagination*, about which a great deal will be said in the second half of this project.

A second acknowledgement is to bear in mind that in choosing the path of managing de-contextualization we have chosen for all. Our universal connectedness is increaseingly threatened by de-contextualization. De-contextualization causes our choices to be less available for analysis, and therefore more random and unassignable, which is to say it will increase the 'disconnect.' As we will demonstrate below, the random, disconnected choices we make will surely have a negative impact on others.

2. Connectedness

In above sections we described how individual choices can bring influence and pressure to bear on the overall ideological systems of an entire society. Our choices therefore lend credence, stability and a degree of certainty to particular dimensions of some current ideology and oppose other dimensions. As already stated, de-contextualization obscures the alternatives, causing choices in thinking processes to become haphazard and appear totally disconnected. This has two important general effects, one psychological and the other societal. Both combine to show a sharp tendency to support the interests of certain segments of the social order and oppose others.

The first effect of disconnectedness, that is, the psychological, is revealed as the disconnectedness perpetuates a mood of isolation and aloneness. Such a mood makes it difficult to connect with others in any meaningful way. This provokes a general social malaise consisting of angst, anger, guilt and depression, moods and attitudes that become the underlying emotional support for social alienation. This makes any attempt at collective planning confused, fragmented, scattered, and therefore conflicted and utterly compromised. Social action and change then comes to appear remote, if not impossible, a view which serves only the interests of an entrenched status quo.

The second general effect of disconnectedness, the societal, is dialectically bound up with the psychological. However, the societal effect can be best understood as a distinct phenomenon when one sees that random and incoherent choices are non-threatening to existing ideologies and therefore tacitly support them. The view and understanding of the existing reality does not simply remain unchallenged, but is actually supported and strengthened by fragmented thinking. Because disconnectedness tends to support existing ideologies it *ipso facto* opposes change and resists the flexibility demanded for contextual awareness. Currently, a lack of change in contextual awareness supports de-contextualization which in turn fosters the disconnectedness and the kind of random and aimless choosing which supports existing ideologies. We can see a cycle here that is both stubborn and elusive.

At the individual level, we need to point out that there are more obvious ways in which individual Situational analysis, and therefore individual Situational ethics, can suffer from de-contextualization. For instance, when you choose, with limited awareness, to be inducted into a religious sect, and thus increase the general pressure for an acceptance of a certain doctrine[xv] or worldview, you

---

[xv] A reminder that 'doctrine' is not the same creature as 'ideology.' Doctrine is a compatible expression of a wider, existing ideological matrix. For example, ancient Egyptian mythology, as a religious doctrine, is not compatible with an existing 21st Century ideological platform, and is therefore a religious doctrine that has been cast aside. Capitalism, as economic doctrine, is compatible with 21st Century ideology, but would have been inexpressible from the ideological platform of Egypt of the Pharaohs.

choose for far more individuals than the members of your sect or party or neighborhood. Again, you universally choose an exclusiveness that augments the disconnectedness and the isolation. To illustrate: As we read these words, both Christianity and Islam come to mind as such doctrinaire forces that argue for a certain slant on the perception of material realities. The greater the number of adherents, and the more extreme the view, the sharper will be the confrontation with a widely diverse number of societies and individuals. In this case, we might consider a clash between the esoteric views of Christianity and Islam.

Much of our socio-cultural atmosphere depends strongly on the choices of world views shared by only a fraction of individuals within that society. Typically, this type of influence spreads overtly rather than obliquely and the effect is felt individually as well a socially. The resulting isolation and alienation causes feeling of hostility to quicken and surface irrationally. The hostility is directed not just at the doctrine fostering the isolation and alienation, but also outward from the doctrine toward the other.

We should note that the above examples carry the underlying precondition that a coherent knowledge initiates and empowers choices that are both fitting and prevailing. By extension, knowledge, information, and the manner in which we organize that knowledge and information, are vital ingredients in our choices and therefore in our universal connectedness. For now it is most important to understand that choice is the material dynamic behind our connection with reality, as well as manifestations of our personal ethics, and this rests on what we have come to know. It is not too difficult to realize that just as choice and our personal ethics are not easily cast aside and ignored, neither can we cast aside our responsibility to overcome de-contextualization through satisfying the underlying pre-condition of accomplished choice – the gathering of an organized and rational knowledge base which opposes de-contextualization. There is no faster route to re-securing universal human connectedness.

Quite a number of philosophers – among the more famous of these we find Kant and Sartre – have previously pointed out that when we choose we choose for our entire species. Although philosophers, such as Kant and Sartre, did not mean precisely the same thing by this claim of choosing for all, we can acknowledge the general similarity of their assertions with the claim offered here.[29] It seems, then, that like responsibility, universal connectedness is also impossible to push aside. As we have shown, there is nothing abstract or spiritual in this connectedness, or the responsibility it implies. Both are quite real. Our con-nection with all in our time and existence (and one might add, connection with all throughout history) is both a material and an ethical reality rather we like it or not. We need only make the following observation: If universal connectedness is a result of the ethical choices we make, and the intrinsic consequences takes the form of the *personal* responsibility we bear for these choices, we must make all of our choices carefully and with the greatest possible knowledge of the context in which we live. This suggestion flies in the face of a de-contextualized socio-political environment. Through a struggle to fully re-connect with our context, we must look to allowing for the possession of the fullest possible grasp on the vulnerability of others. In this sense, our Situational ethical standard may shield us from the greatest measure of guilt that seems inherent in our existential predicament.

Given what has been said above, it should come as no surprise that universal responsibility is ours. This has been clearly implied throughout the discussion of Situational ethics. Responsibility is perhaps the most important point of this section on ethics, if for only the single reason that it fittingly segues well into the Situational question of "What can I do about this world?!"

WHAT CAN I DO?

The true test for the Situational ethic is found in the question: What Can I Do? This is an honest, forthright and angry question; for what are we to do in the face of overwhelming frustration? It seems everywhere we turn there exists a jungle of horrors – war, economic exploitation, rising sea levels, world-wide famine, natural disaster and epidemic disease, and on and on, seemingly without end. Can the human species outrun its extinction?

The world is an overwhelming place and the events frequently strange in their menace and disfiguring in their vagueness. The issues appear not just confusing, but exist on a scope that completely dwarfs the individual. When I look at the choices, at the possible effects of my small contribution, 'What Can I Do?' is a question that stares back at me, bleak and resonating in its apparent hopelessness.

I use the 'I' above in the collective sense. I do not mean the 'I' as in 'Me,' – I intend the 'I' to mean the I-collectively! That is to say the 'We!' Although this project in intended to focus on the individual "I," it cannot be overlooked that it is We, all of us, who are caught up in this troubled world. It is We who made the human world. It is We who are responsible for it and its state.[xvi] For a variety of reasons some of us seem immune to its effects, but all of

---

[xvi] As mentioned in the introduction, and elsewhere, the issue of an entire society being organized along the lines of Situational ethics might well be possible, and practical. This is, however, an issue for another project. Here we are focused on the individual and not the political order.

us see this world in its shocking reality. As it is We (I-collectively) who are responsible, it is We who must get ourselves out of this troubled place. There are no miracles that will suddenly come upon the world like a clap of thunder and save us all. There is only the I-collective and much work...an endless and universal amount of work. We suspect this is so, and like the Sword of Damocles the naked question hangs above us all: "What Can I Do?"

There is an answer to the question, "What Can I Do?" There is an answer that by its nature will fit every Situation. This sounds odd, if not impossible. It is true and not even terribly complicated. The answer is not rarefied, or God centered. Nor is the answer the private terrain of the gifted, the powerfully placed, or the genius. A complete answer to the question 'What Can I Do?' is available to everyone. But as the answer does require a discussion of the question before its availability will make any sense. So before directly tackling an answer to the question of 'What Can I Do?' we must to do this little bit of ground work.

"What Can I Do?" This question dangles at eye level, just off to the side, annoyingly in peripheral sight, always vaguely there. About the first thing that should strike us is that this is a question asked more often by the young than the old. That the young ask more often, and with greater insistence, is an important clue to making sense of the question. We correctly suspect that the old have grown cynical and immune to the horrors. This gives the young the impression that the old have grown gnarled and conservative in their dotage. 'Grown conservative' is a not the best interpretation of this very human response. For the mature, their personal history of the world is draped like layers of hardened shock over their sense of things they have witnessed. Their defense against the world is to seal the doorway to their conscience. Cynicism is a protective devise, albeit an ugly one.

It is difficult to live forty plus years and find fault with rational individuals for giving up on a rational search for the answers to problems that confound our species. We reflexively turn away from the pain. Staying focused on the world's ugly problems is difficult. We turn to distraction, to entertainment, go shopping, and search for solace in spiritual ideology. In the face of overwhelming issues experience has taught the old to turn away from the big picture and like Voltaire's *Candide*, tend exclusively to their own garden. This is how the mature mind adjusts to their personal post-traumatic syndrome. The mind stops dreaming and turns inward. Is this private and narcissistic turn not the best, and safest, of all possible worlds?

Searching out the nature of how the mature have learned to cope opens us to the three basic issues involved in adjustment to the world: (1) *Cynicism*, which does have a positive side; (2) *ideology*, which is much larger than mere politics; and (3) *scope*, to focus on the size of the problem, or alternatively, the smallness of the individual. To the casual eye these three issues appear dissimilar, yet they are not. Together, or separately, they serve to present a wall that defends us against responsibility and guilt. These devises also wall us off from realizing that our tiny individuality can break new ground, that we can make a significant difference. Thus, it also walls us off from a fear of cowardice. Let us take a moment to examine the brick and mortar of that wall.

Cynicism. An interesting consideration of cynicism is to reflect on it as a type of angry wisdom. This is both a wisdom and an anger derived from the genuine care we extend to what goes on in the world…and also the powerlessness we feel. As we will note, cynicism is a dark cloud with an oddly limitless silver lining. People without a cynical side are either the very young or the relatively untouched, either that or they are people who have learned to care about events around them with an extreme and biting sense of caution.

To despair is to have been touched. Despair is a normal psychological response to an ugly context that is both shocking to ordinary human decency and at the same time seems at the edge of any pale of hope. It is when the terrible sights and sounds sweep beyond this pale that we must protect ourselves from the ensuing despair, least it submerge us in dark depression. We suffer a kind of information overload and either turns away completely out of shock and disgust, or quietly feel the despair become the first crust of cynicism.

The direction we choose, either turning to the distractions in the world, and in a sense to choose to be unconscious of the world, or turning to cynicism as an intellectually charged shield against despair, is determined differently by every person. For those individuals who cannot find peace in confronting the world, cynicism is the most likely dam against the ensuing onslaught. All things considered, we must conclude that cynicism is not a sign of shallowness, but the opposite, a bittersweet sign of depth.

Cynicism is a sign of consciousness, and in this case a sign of a social consciousness, albeit one gone astray. Through cynicism, even that type gone awry, social consciousness begins to spark symptoms of an emerging political consciousness.

Ideology. As a general rule, we tend to think of ideology as a rationalizing element of political propaganda, and the ideologue as a 'front man' for a political party or a mountebank hawking a political doctrine – one is a Christian-Democrat, a Republican, a prompter of Socialism, etc. We show a tendency to consider ideology as either some underlying diatribe for political warfare or arising as a direct result of political theory. All this puts the cart before the horse. Ideology is much broader than politics. Ideology is a historically derived, *total idea-system* at work throughout a particular time and place. Ideology is the more or less organized thinking patterns we use to interpret and mediate the reality at work between our social world and ourselves. Ideology is what goes on in our heads that allow us to make sense of what we see around us and allow us shelter from the 'mysterious' occurrences in our environment, both natural and social. Many ideologies have political dimensions and implications, but ideologies, in and of themselves, are not only political.

For example, during the 13th century we might see children wasting of an unknown malady. The ideas system available to us at that time fit this pestilence into a spiritual system of witches and demons as part of the struggle between God and the devil, something beyond mere human intervention. Look! The red splotches on the child show the mark of the devil! Do we not see what we see? Yes, but while we see the splotches on the child's skin, what we actually 'see' before us are the limits of medieval, super-natural ideology.

Or more currently, we might witness violent dislocations in the financial system and through the lens of ideology see it as the 'natural rhythm' of the marketplace and again beyond the reach of human intervention. Or we might see famine and pestilence in far off corners of the world and determine it to be 'necessarily' Malthusian or evolutionary adjustments, and simply beyond human control. In a wink, we can see that a good many idea-systems serve to protect us from responsibility. Obviously, for us here in the contemporary world, some explanations are more realistic than others, that is, some idea-systems allow for a more accurate reading of the events in our world than do others. Clearly, a scientific ideology will read the red splotches on a child's body in a far more accurate manner than a metaphysical idea-system churning out medieval superstition.

Though the origin of the idea-systems we call ideology is beyond the scope of this essay, we can say that, in general, the systems are the dynamic result of conflict between ideas, the new verses the old. That is, the ideas in our heads are the result of ideas already in general acceptance as they are adjusted by new questions posed by practical, material reality. The greater the input of ex-perience and information the greater the complexity of the outcome; that is, the more refined the experience the more radical the impact on idea-systems. But again, the point being made here is that ideology can act as one of the less than conscious defenses against human responsibility – or act as a standard bearer for forces advancing human possibilities and potential. To some great extent, this is a matter of choice.

Scope. The individual is immediately confronted by the breadth and depth of a complex, worldwide-picture. The magnitude of any problem can appear overwhelming, especially when taken in as a whole. But, ideology aside, at some level we are aware that human beings had a hand in nearly all the problems we see and therefore human beings can begin solving the problems. Yet, the sheer magnitude of the issues deflects us, causes us to turn away, retreat from the historical and human dimensions of the forces at hand. All is too big and we are too small. We are confronted with something of an existential Gordian Knot – but for us there is no hero, no Alexander to slice through the knot. The swing of the sword is left up to 'We.' So, what do 'We' possess that can cut through the Knot?

In the above sections on "Situational Ethics" we discussed at great length the relationship of knowledge to how we see the world and how knowledge affects the nature of our choices. We choose and behave according to our knowledge of the alternatives existing within Situations. We choose to do one thing or the other according to our understanding of the alternatives. If our understanding is incomplete or just plain wrong, we will not choose the best option. In this case a poor choice will not only be an issue for the chooser, a poor choice that will mostly likely generate problems for others.

Actions do not occur in a vacuum. If you choose to drink and drive, to donate blood, to cheat on your taxes, or volunteer at a local school, all will have an impact on others around you, many of who will very often be people you do not know and will never know. This makes even the casual choices we all make of greater moment than we usually give them credit for. This Gordian Knot that is our world exists of dimensions we could hardly suspect.

Like Alexander, we cut through the Knot by making incisive decisions based *first* on an accurate accounting of the Situation and *second,* grasping the measure of the impact made by a choice and the depth of our personal responsibility for having made it. This hardly represents new thinking, but it serves to underscore that having a correct grasp on reality is fundamental to arriving at correct decisions. All this is very abstract. This section of the project is meant to leave abstractions behind and move forward toward practical, everyday answers for the choices faced by the individual confronting personal Situations.

In order to accomplish this, it is necessary to face an unvarnished and unbalanced reality without apology. Some harsh and blunt things will have to be said and examined. At times, we will have to be guided purely by our suspicions of imbalance. That is, we will have to be guided by that lack of proportionality discussed in the section above on the impact of the Situation. We must be both sensitive and unafraid to forcefully declare an absence of balance in the Situation at-hand.

A Personal Question and Answer.

The question: As an average human being, what can I do to make a meaningful and positive change in my society and in the world at large? At one time or another we have all asked this question, or one very much like it.

For most of us it has been a question raised and then dismissed because of the seeming impossibility of a practical, everyday answer. If you are one that has chosen to drop the question because of its overwhelming scope you would have been too hasty. There is a pragmatic, real world reply to this question. The answer can be uncovered through a process of closely observing and analyzing your particular landscape – that is, your particular place both *on* and *in* this plane of reality, that is, your *Situation*.[xvii] This place, your Situation, is unique. It is a Situation that no other person shares. Everyone occupies a different place in this 'landscape,' as we may refer to your personal context. Through analysis, your unique Situation offers to you a vantage point that will tell you precisely why this, your Situation, is either appropriate to positively affect the elements of contextual reality around you, or tell you what is preventing you from affecting change in your landscape. This analysis will offer you a handle on what needs to be done to change your position in order that you may achieve greater effectiveness in treating the elements of this landscape, that is, your personal context within this material reality – again, your Situation.

By 'position' it is meant both the physical and existential place in which you find yourself. Your personal landscape has both physical and intellectual dimensions. They greatly influence each other and are not at all mutually exclusive. In this project we will focus on the intellectual and existential dimensions. Locating the im-

---

[xvii] The term 'Situation' is described and analyzed above in the section titled "The Situation."

portance of your physical placement in your landscape will tend to follow as relevance demands.

The above is a mouthful of words. It can be briefly summed up in two considerations. First, you'll notice that all the talk of context and placement can be rewritten in two words: *Change yourself.* As we roll this expression around in our minds it has the dissatisfying ring of a cliché. However, the notion of a cliché only implies an adage that has become trite through its mundane obviousness, not necessarily its lack of truth. As we proceed in the remainder of this project we will see that changing yourself is far more than a cliché. This will become increasing clear.

Second, this phrase, *change yourself*, also appears a dead end. The phrase offers no directional hints, no guideposts to help you along the road of change. It seems just another disappointing and hollow platitude. The phrase, *change yourself*, as used here, therefore needs some elaboration. However, even a through unpacking process requires some explanation.

To change the way you are is to change your Situation within the context in which you find yourself. Before any change can take place there must be a grasp on what underlies your personal Situation. This understanding starts with what should be apparent: Where you find yourself at the moment of being born is a tossing into this reality by pure random happenstance.[xviii] There is no reason for you to have been flung into this place as opposed to that place. In fact, there is no reason for You. We must

---

[xviii] If you have chosen to read this part of the book first, this rather startling remark about being tossed was described and explained at some length in the previous section on ethics. A re-analysis here will be brief.

recognize this, and if this comes as a fearful understanding, it is also an empowering understanding. You are merely a random event and that random event makes change not just possible, but *inevitable*, and *impossible to avoid*. This is empowerment. This realization is your starting point.

Only at birth are the material strictures of your position in this wide stream of historical circumstance beyond your control. Your arrival is a gross contingency. Where you find yourself in the landscape in the beginning, both historically and geographically, is your primal circumstance. Who your birth parents are, the social position of your family, your cultural matrix, and where on this planet you have found yourself, are also random actualities, and primal, but like the runner at the starting block of a foot race you are fixed and powerless only at that single, precise moment. Your arrival leaves no eternal mark. These primal circumstances are fixed only at the moment of your tossing. Thereafter, and increasingly, the position of where you find yourself in the landscape is a matter of free choice – your Situation becomes your freedom, and also your responsibility. You may not be able to do anything about the event of your tossing, but the remaining events in your life, though shaded by the original tossing, are steadily circumstances of which you are the creator.

Do you want meaningful change? As you read these words you must recognize that all that is You, within the strictures of the historical, material reality, have been your choice from the tossing and therefore your responsibility. Without this conscious awareness about yourself and your Situation any answer to the question 'what can I do about this world?' will never be satisfactory or complete; the answer will forever be elusive and you powerless. There is then a two part answer to the question, 'What Can I Do?'

At the beginning, realize first and foremost, there exists your sense of Being, which is to say your raw consciousness. Beyond that, you are the only creator for who you are and the foundation for that creation. This position has been our argument throughout this project. Your consciousness is your only foundation for recreating who you are and choosing your Situation. What is of immediate relevance is *first* a change in consciousness, and a particular kind of consciousness at that. This raises many questions concerning the nature of consciousness. Presently, we will look at consciousness in detail.

Second, a complete understanding of the power relations in the world is what you must possess in order that you are in a position to create positive changes. 'What Can I Do?' runs smack into the face of worldly power. It demands an understanding that fully grasps the issues of power on both a small and large scale. This shift does not involve changing your personality, but only a facet of your awareness of your individual power vis-à-vis the world of power. Now, I think we can begin to see that the Situation in which we find ourselves is manageable, even if at this point it still seems a little abstract.

As suggested above, and before going any further, it is necessary to discuss, in some detail, the two topics that both frame and infiltrate the question of, 'What Can I Do?' We speak of consciousness and power. A firm grasp of these two topics is vital to taking a first step to a change in your landscape, that is, impact your individual Situation.

Both the topics of human consciousness and real world power enframe and saturate any proposed development for positive change, and they are related, as we will see.

The Nature of Consciousness.

To begin with, consciousness is different than awareness, and we ought not to get the two confused. Consciousness and awareness are both present in our common humanity as brute fact, but are still quite distinct.[30] Awareness and consciousness, as in the common Venn diagram, overlap in many places, just as do most of our other animal and human characteristics. Therefore, consciousness and awareness bear a strong affinity for each other. They are, however, different entities, just as are our animal and human attributes. Of the two, consciousness is more difficult to describe than awareness, but in contrasting the two a greater understanding of consciousness will emerge.

I am going to make the claim that awareness is hardwired directly in that neurological part of our animal physicality. The hardwiring for awareness is designed, as it is for all animals, for the survival and healthy continuance of life. Awareness is not a reflective reaction, it is a sentient reaction. Awareness is an auto response that is largely triggered by our baseline biological drives for survival and procreation. Thus, the awareness response, like the raw animal instinct for survival, cannot be classified as good or bad, right or wrong, because it simply is.

In taking a hard look at consciousness, we will see that there is only the *capacity* for consciousness hard wired into our common human physicality. Unlike survival, there is nothing instinctual or automatic about consciousness. We merely possess the neural circuitry to afford a base level for consciousness. Consciousness has features such as focus and reflection that are distinctly human dispositions, yet must be developed from the raw aptitude. For example, we are born with a readiness to reflect, but not with the capability. Infants, as nearly as we can tell, do not reflect on the nature of the source of their nourishment and protective warmth. Reflection speaks of consciousness,[31] but reflection is only the cultivation of proclivities found within the potential for consciousness. Consciousness is a refinement of neural disposition, and must be continued to be refined throughout our lives. This means that consciousness can take place on many levels, an important feature that will have greater meaning during the following discussions.

It is awareness rather than consciousness that possess the elements of instinct for survival. Consciousness, on the other hand, can enhance awareness through reflection on what is awareness, yet by the nature of reflection it stands apart in a posture of 'looking.' Consciousness functions in tandem to awareness but cannot produce awareness. Certain types of awareness can bring an enhancement to consciousness. This is a rare event, and something we will delve into later. For now, let us just say that awareness and consciousness come from the same human fact, but serve that humanity in distinct ways.

Both 'awareness' and 'consciousness' have an identical starting physicality: The neural gestalt of the central nervous system, (i.e., the brain). After this jumping off point, the two (awareness and consciousness), while tangled, develop separately and uniquely, and afford us different service. It is easy for us to understand that our 'sentient reaction' is a product of certain bio-chemical reactions interwoven into our central nervous system. In addition, we understand that a 'survival instinct' (i.e., as an awareness reaction) is part of our mental design that we share with nearly all animals. As stated above, this survival instinct is neither good nor bad. The survival instinct merely is. Consciousness, while very frequently provoked by awareness, is something apart from both sentient awareness and survival instinct. We have an internal understanding that consciousness is something 'higher' than awareness. This is not to say that consciousness is something 'metaphysical,' but rather something telescoped, broader and deeper, networked, an encompassing reflecting thing that is uniquely human and not shared with animals. For example, I have no trouble saying that my dog is aware of my presence in the room. I am certainly part of her sense of well-being and survival. However, there is a slight hesitation in saying that my dog is conscious of me. To say 'conscious' would imply that the dog has a separate, abstract sense of me apart from my immediate presence in the room.[32] To be conscious implies something more than what we suspect animals of being capable. I, on the other hand, can be both aware of my dog in the room, and at the same time be conscious of her in a more abstract sense.

Here is the clear and important and defining difference between the two. To be aware is a *passive* process. To say that we are *aware* is to say that 'things' outside of us are happening to us. Awareness knocks up against us and puts my sense of well-being on alert. To be conscious is an *active* process. When we are conscious we are engaged with things. We are extended into a host of things and events both inside and outside of ourselves in a pro-active way. There is something about us that is happening to things. Those 'things' can be outside, can be material, as when we consciously consider a tree, another person, or clouds. These 'things' can also be internal products of my mind, as when we consider the abstractions of love, or happiness – or human rights versus governmental power. This does *not* mean that something like our happiness can *not* have a concrete dialectical *expression* outside of us – for example, the person I love as both the provocation *and* the object of my love. Awareness alone can clearly stimulate conscious interest, as in the arousal of a sexual interest, but awareness does not guide me to feel love; clearly love and sexual interest can be related, but are not identical. Sexual arousal is a part of instinctual interest while love is a conscious development, and is only sometimes related to sexual arousal. To offer another perspective, we can say that happiness has no *meaning* outside of our conscious (or perhaps subconscious) connection with a person (even ourselves), a thing or an event. Happiness is an engaged process, a 'conscious' deportment of my mind. We are conscious of happiness rather than being aware of it.

Consciousness and Curiosity. Consciousness also discloses its distinct shape along the line of focused, intentional curiosity. Nothing about our intentionality suggests consciousness so much as does curiosity. Intentional curiosity is part of this engaging syndrome marking the human consciousness. Although this curiosity is a developmental manifestation of the instinct to survive, as we will see, no other creature possesses a curiosity with *intent*. Curiosity doesn't always kill the cat. More often it is the provider of knowledge that saves the cat. Curiosity very often opens doors that promote life and well-being. It is hard to imagine us surviving as humans beings without curiosity. Curiosity is so deeply involved in the awakening and deployment of consciousness that it is sometimes difficult to separate the two. Ironically, this deployment of consciousness through curiosity might be an entirely unconscious process, a kind of deeply human efficacy without any obvious personal sense of involvement through a direct sense of purpose.[33] Oddly, human curiosity can be intentional without being immediately purposeful.

Of course, many animals show a keen interest in things found in their immediate environment. They do exhibit behaviors that are sometimes referred to as 'curiosity.' But this behavior is not *intentional* on the part of animals. They are engaged, or if you will, seized from without by things and events having direct relationship to aspects of their well-being, (e.g., food); they do not reach out, but are seized from without. And of course, to suggest that animals other than humans have a special, intentional curiosity about such things as the nature of clouds, the history of their species, magic, or any other abstraction, is absurd. Engagement with the abstract is a result of intentional curiosity, a human trait, even if piqued by outside events or things. 'Intentionality,' as a part of a curiosity syndrome, is suited only to human consciousness. This syndrome is a coincidental set of thoughts that probe and engage things outside of the conscious mind. The syndrome of engagement is meant to satisfy some internal impulse that is ultimately traceable to a fulfillment of well-being. Lesser animals are aware, but not conscious; they are engaged rather than engaging.

All animals have senses that are receptive to stimulation from the world around them, a receptiveness that is the neurological pathway to a sentient reaction. As stated above, we hold that this awareness is quite distinguishable from 'consciousness,' just as instincts for survival and well-being are distinct from the development of abstract curiosity or a curiosity syndrome. However, survival and the curiosity syndrome are related in the sense that the instinct for survival is the trigger for this syndrome, abstract and otherwise. We can be comfortable about saying that animals show a 'curious' interest in immediate food sources, but no such 'curious' interest in the abstract habits of predators – their mating rituals, or foraging range, etc. Animals are certainly aware of predators, but to say they are 'curious' about them is a stretch too far. Humans, on the other hand, are very likely to show a great curiosity about the nature and habits of predators – especially the human kind – recognizing that these habits can be intimately related to physical, social, legal, or economic survival.

The ultimate manifestations of curiosity may appear so remote from instincts for survival, or the human ontology of Being,[xix] that any connection can seem tenuous at best. For example, what can I say about my curiosity surrounding what might lay beneath the ice mantel on Jupiter's moon, Europa?[34] A bit of reflection will reveal

---

[xix] See the above section *Vulnerability As An Ontological Link*, p. 63

that such curiosity could easily relate to questions regarding the origins of life in this our universe, which can ultimately be traced to authentic ontological bafflements, such as: "In all this space, why me?" In nearly all cases, a rearward looking analysis will trace even idle curiosity to either factors originating in our universal need to avoid (*survive?*) death, or a need for well-being in its most ontic sense, which can be shown to be linked to a resolution of the general ontological puzzlement surrounding our existence. As strange as it might sound at first, it might even be argued that self-awareness of both existence and the end of existence (i.e., death) are two of the most important universal instigators for the expansion of human consciousness, as well as the foundation for our sense of curiosity. If nothing else, this link to our own individual 'primal circumstance,'[xx] and our ultimate end, shows that the expansion of consciousness need not be traced to anything esoteric or even abstract, but is solidly rooted in existence and survival awareness.

None of what has been said above is to be construed to mean that awareness is a secondary factor to consciousness, or is less important. While awareness and consciousness are related, independent awareness can be a powerful force on its own, and occasionally a force of great moment for humans. It is fair to say that awareness and consciousness very often act in concert, like two individual people on a dance floor, with awareness frequently the leader of the dance team. This image suggests an important

---

[xx] See the above chapter 'The Situation' (p.1). In fact, be reminded that much of the groundwork for this section was established in the above section.

insight: Awareness can provoke sudden shifts in consciousness. Certain powerful events of awareness can trip a powerful curiosity response in consciousness. This is a key consideration when struck with the facts of the world, provoking an intimate reaching out with 'What Can I Do?' Awareness can impact people in such a way as to force sudden and compelling changes in consciousness. In a manner of speaking, awareness can flip the switch on the preverbal 'light bulb,' unexpectedly, and often with virulence. However, the 'light bulb' itself is consciousness being lit by curiosity.

To say that I am 'conscious' is to suggest that something about my Being[xxi] is *active* rather than *passive*. Consciousness is that part of my Being that actively 'reaches out to engage' things beyond me, beyond my individual state. As already discussed, this 'reaching out to engage' is driven by that basic human ability to be curious, which draws it energy and design from one of the many manifestations of survival and of a deep and universal need for 'well-being,' both physical well-being and, if I may, existential well-being. As all of these many elements of humanness are embedded in human physicality, they are universal among our species. That being stressed, we move on to point out that this 'reaching-out,' this curiosity, is aided by another human characteristic: *Focus*.

Focus and Reflection: Human consciousness, in the form of curiosity, motivates and shapes this thing we call focus, this willful, intentional 'reaching out.' As curiosity

---

[xxi] In the use of the concept Being, I mean to indicate 'me' as the primal circumstance, a raw facticity separate from the determining factors of time and place. Being is the 'I' as a brute and independent fact.

– which directs consciousness outward – becomes ever more acute and energized by some level of well-being, so the focus intensifies. To say that I 'direct consciousness outward' or 'reaching out' does not necessarily mean a reaching toward something outside of my individual being, but only toward a thing distinguishable from my sense of Being, *per se*. I can focus (i.e., aim) my consciousness on internal things as well as external things, at my sense of focus itself, for example, for the purpose of *reflection*. I can also focus consciousness on itself in what we typically call 'self-consciousness.'

This thing, this *focus*, is an intentional or willful act: I *intend* to do this thing; I *intend* to do that thing. To say that I *intend* is also to acknowledge that I have an understanding of future time. This recognition of time is yet another novel human 'understanding,'[35] and again, this understanding of time is quite probably rooted in the 'end of time,' which is to say, our own death, also related to well-being. Nearly every uniquely human quality, it seems, is ultimately embedded in questions concerning the origin of life, or its continuance (i.e., well-being) – questions, which in and of themselves, possess no objective ethical claims.

Focus goes beyond reaching out to a thing. Focus, as part of the curiosity syndrome, acts to *envelope* a thing. Focus, as an intentional act, is a tool of consciousness that envelops the thing aimed at by curiosity, and then separates this thing from the surrounding environment, then draws it inward for an internal viewing. The separation we will call *uncovering* and the internal viewing *reflection*. This last – reflection – is derived from another singular human capability: The *imaginative* ability to employ *reason* to arrange and rearrange complex patterns into a *revealing* of meaning.[36] Imagination, reason and reflection are nothing magical, they originate with our natural hardwiring, that ability built into our neurological gestalt, and are available to everyone. Only this ability must possess things previously revealed which is to act as a reflecting surface. Reflection is the bouncing of the enveloped thing off internal things (as abstractions) previously revealed, often by an absorbing ideology – transforming them into abstract entities eventually to be integrated and secured in the intellectual gestalt. For the sake of simplicity we will call this integration *knowledge*. In this context, one might say that reflection acts very like an internal pinball machine, reflecting previously known things off introduced abstract entities, shaping through the use of reason and imagination until the perfect slot is found or developed. The development and nature of these slots increases the overall growth and stability of an expanding intellect – and expanding consciousness.

We must be very careful, however, for we cannot say that this thing called knowledge is necessarily accurate or materially correct in any truly objective sense. Knowledge is always limited by both language and ideology. But of the two, language is more deliberately controlled by conscious development and direction, making ideology the greater hindrance.[37] The reflective qualities that shape 'knowledge' is, of necessity, part of the ideological atmosphere into which we were thrown; the knowledge may only reflect the nature of the ideological platform. For example, before the development of a rigorous science (a relatively new ideology!) we knew many things. We knew, for example that the sun revolved around the earth, and that royalty reigned by the will of God, and that the earth was flat, and so on. Our ideology underwrote this integration of reflection, this knowledge, and more, our ideology told us that all these things were true beyond any reasonable doubt. In fact, 'doubt' itself is part of a much newer and expanded ideological platform – only a few hundred years old – an idea platform that never existed until the end of the 'Age of Faith.' We must always remember that what we 'know' is always 'suspect,' and beholding to the current ideological soil in which all 'knowledge' is ultimately rooted.

The ability to reflect also possesses a *willful* (as intentional) element, and is both a tool of curiosity and a result of consciousness. The precise origin of will is, for now, uncertain,[38] but it is clear that will (and intent) exists tangentially to our ability to reflect, and reflection is a development of 'understanding' which is rooted in knowing. Will and reflection are powerful tools in a human arsenal that augments instinctual survival and well-being to a level much higher than that experienced by the other animals. More pointedly, these tools are what make us unquestionably human, for only humans have the capacity to *know* in the abstract sense (i.e., to hold reflection in suspension.)

So, consciousness is not merely the reaching out to things, but also, by the medium of focus, consciousness is the drawing-in of things for an extensive search and *grasp* of the uncovered, which leads to the *revelation* of meaning through intentional reflection. Focus is a proactive tool of consciousness, sparked by curiosity, designed to envelope and remove things from background clutter. Focus allows for intentional reflection and manipulation. Meaning is revealed, and advanced, through willful envelopment and manipulation by those things that we already know. Thus, I advance the uncovered by 'reflecting' the uncovered off the mirror of my *previously established knowledge*, guiding it toward the appropriate slot in my intellectual framework. This framework expands and develops according to the level of dedication applied to the process described.

To make an understanding of the interplay of awareness, curiosity and reflection more concrete, let me offer an illustration. A deer may become *aware* of wolves in the vicinity. Awareness is the alertness, the ringing of the survival bell. The deer's well-being is clearly at issue. At this point, evolutionary programmed instincts take over the deer's behavior as the deer reacts to those things acting on it. The deer is not curious about the wolves; the deer does not direct a reflection on the meaning of the wolves, or reflect on what it knows about the behavior of the wolves (indeed, if it truly *knows* anything about wolves in some abstract sense) nor does it consider alternative actions regarding the wolves. Evolution has set the deer on a different survival course than the survival course set for humans. The deer is aware, rather than conscious, of the wolves and merely reacts within the limited scope that evolutionary instinct has provided. A human, once made aware, can make an internal switch from passive to active, can exhibit curiosity, and can reach out to the wolves with intentional focus. That is to say, a human being can direct con-sciousness in a probing way at the meaning of the wolves, and then can 'reflect,' which is to say, climb across the web of knowledge the individual possesses about the wolves, and then choose a course of action based on a variety of alternative actions abstractly known about the wolves and the Situation. It is clear that these proactive elements of focus, curiosity and reflection, which are adjunctive tools of consciousness, are factors uniquely human.

Yet, even given the originality offered by humanness there exists only the *possibility* that willful focus and reflection can happen. Innate human reactions can be overridden by an existing ideology so as to short-circuit reflection and cause instinctual reflexes to be misdirected. For example, from the Aztecs to the Christians, the victims of the many forms of human sacrifice have overridden their natural survival instincts and quite often gone willingly to their deaths. Such is the power of ideology, thus demonstrating that effective, intentional reflection guiding our behavior is only one *possibility* for our species.

For us humans, consciousness is the following: Consciousness is both our human tool that separates, and is the cause of our human separation from the world. All of the tools of consciousness – curiosity, imagination and reflection, *et. al.* – a mixture we might lump together under the heading of *thinking* – serves the ends of separation, as well as the angst separation provokes. The tools of consciousness, and therefore consciousness itself, allow us to survive as individuals, but at the awesome cost of separation and aloneness. Consciousness is the active reaching out to engage, to remove the object of curiosity (which can be 'us') from the background, to pull the object in for a reflection, a re-fitting and warehousing. With focus and consciousness we separate things from the noisy pool and the background clutter for reflection and study. With self-consciousness we separate ourselves forever from the din and the mix of reality; self-consciousness is our pure aloneness, our purest sense of isolation. However, while this conscious-ness is a defining characteristic human alienation, it is at the same time an incessant inclination toward the practical business of survival and well-being. But to be truly productive consciousness must be honed and refined and strengthened. To be truly effective consciousness must be expanded.

The task ahead in finding answer to our question of 'What Can I Do?' is to look considerably more deeply into this expansion of consciousness. How do we cause consciousness to expand enough to envelope ever larger and more complex entities so that a practical answer to the question 'What Can I Do?' can be revealed?

Raising Consciousness in General.

Above, the descriptive term used was 'expanding consciousness.' We will now switch to the phrase *raising consciousness*.[xxii] Considering the way we will approach this subject the term 'raising consciousness' not only implies something positive, but is also more descriptively appropriate. From a higher position of consciousness, one can get a much wider and deeper perspective on both the historical context and the immediate landscape. At the

---

[xxii] 'Raising consciousness' is frequently used to indicate a specific type of political development. For the moment, we will ignore this meaning of the term.

same time that consciousness is elevated it can also reach out further and take in larger envelopments for reflection. This establishes a cycle that willfully raises consciousness even higher. There is nothing magical in this raising of consciousness. Nor is it something available only to the blessed few, as in some sort of intellectual elite. Raising consciousness is largely a matter of individual choice, a choice available for us all, an action based on more fully grasping the material world inhabited by all of us. It needs to be stressed that as a choice, raising consciousness is more than an action 'available' to everyone; raising consciousness is a *responsibility* for everyone who wants to claim the title of human being.

If the raising of human consciousness turns on the development of an intellect framework designed for reflection, as it clearly seems to do, then the raising of consciousness must be part of a process concerned with the *augmentation* of experience. This word augmentation is employed here judiciously, for augmentation of experience is not the same thing as simply learning more, although 'learning more' is a necessary ingredient of the augmentation process. Augmentation of experience, in the way the phrase is used here, is part of a process leading to the unveiling of 'meaning' rather than a technique for warehousing information, though this also has its place. The unveiling of meaning is, at least in one important sense, the conversion of experienced into knowledge.

The raising of consciousness presents a far more delicate arrangement of the intellectual pieces integrated into the framework of envelopment and reflection. Being always mindful of the influence of mainstream ideology, the intellectual framework upon which the raising of consciousness depends must be arranged in such a way as to make two things possible: (1) to make the envelopment conform to a relevant reality and (2) to facilitate a knowledge matrix demanded by precise reflection. This arrangement is not so easily accomplished. The reading of another book is a helpful activity in the development of such an intellectual framework, but is clearly far from a complete answer. A discussion of these factors in total, and why the arrangement of these factors is so difficult, is the first task.

An example will provide a broad descriptive basis as to the development of this intellectual framework. Consider the solar eclipse. Today, in the modern world, we think very little about the mechanics of an eclipse. A solar eclipse, while an awesome spectacle, is not a mysterious or supernatural event. Modern scientific ideology has freed up much of our intellectual abilities. We also know that this freedom of intellect was not always so. While astronomers have, for a very long time, had a realistic grasp on the principles surrounding a solar eclipse, for the human population at-large, trapped in the grip of a supernatural ideology, an eclipse had definite overtones of direct spiritual intervention. An incident involving the pre-Socratic philosopher, Thales of Miletus (ca. 624-546, BCE), serves to both illustrate this point and show the arrangement of the intellectual framework required for envelopment and reflection.

It is reported by Herodotus that Thales successfully predicted a solar eclipse in 585 BCE (modern astronomers place the date at May 28, 585 BCE).[39] On that date there was a battle raging between the Medians and the Lydians. On seeing the eclipse both armies threw down their weapons and refused to fight, the soldiers believing that the eclipse was of supernatural origin and showed divine disapproval with the bloodletting. This event ended a bitter five-year war between the two states. What does this circumstance tell us? Above all else it tells us that the masses of the army and their rulers were superstitious enough to think that the solar eclipse was a sign from their gods. Thales understood the event in other terms. For one thing, this serves to demonstrate that there existed two very different grasps on reality promoted by two different idea-systems. The ideology supporting Thales' intellectual framework was not just different, but allowed for a more accurate picture of a universal reality. This leads us to say that Thales' consciousness was functioning on a 'higher' level than that of the army and its generals. In getting to understand Thales' grasp, we can come to grips with the intellectual framework leading to his correct interpretation of reality as opposed to the masses of Medians and Lydians whose ideology led them to an incorrect interpretation.

We know from historical writings that Thales tended to explain natural phenomena using rational principles as opposed to supernatural principles. This ran counter to the ideological order of the day, an order that consistently advanced supernatural explanations for natural events. Thales was able to step outside of and reject the prevailing idea-system (ideology.) We also know that Thales had a good working knowledge of geometry. We do not know of the exact methods he used, but he was certainly aware of solar eclipses as they occur worldwide at different places for different observers at least twice a year. He also knew of their relation to the cycle of the new moon. This is enough information to give him a jumping off point. As opposed to the empirical observations made by Thales, the average person of his day would have had no tools other than superstition to reveal the meaning of an eclipse. Thales possessed a store of knowledge that provoked a consciousness not widely available at the time.

What can we learn from Thales about revealing the meaning of things? What is it that is involved in the development of Thales' intellectual framework that allowed for a greater accuracy in his grasp of reality? How is the example of Thales relevant to the consciousness achievable by all human beings? To begin with, there are four identifiable factors presented to us in this simple illustration. The first two are inherent to universal human physicality: (1) The ability to reason; (2) the ability to accumulate and collate empirical data, or knowledge. The last two, (3) curiosity and (4) imagination are also inherent as a proclivity found in human hardwiring. But they are also more than simple neural networking. They are *derived* from the *human condition*. Again there is nothing transcendental about these qualities. For Thales, as for the rest of us, these qualities personally can bosom from the material and practical circumstances in which humanity has always found itself. These qualities are available to all.

The details:

(1) The first, **reason**, is the stringing together of entities in a complimentary pattern that accurately reflect the issue under consideration. This is a very human attribute and is obviously a ramification made possible by

- 131 -

human neural circuitry. Thus, it should be obvious that the ability to reason is possessed by all humanity.

(2) The second factor is that of **knowledge,** which is the re-fitting and warehousing of experience. Generally, this re-fitting is the conversion of experience into some form of 'meaning.' This depends on sentient, empirical observation *and* a coherent idea-system. Useful and pragmatic knowledge rests on the conviction that the things that are witnessed occur in the real and physical world and not in some supernatural world. It goes without saying that accuracy of witness depends a great deal on being able to discard suffocating arcane and unrealistic ideologies.

(3) The third factor, **curiosity**, as was discussed above, is rooted in the instinct for survival and well-being. How can we survive best and avoid being eaten? All animals share the automatic instinctive responses for survival. What is different for humanity is that curiosity is not automatic, but an expanded response; it is active rather than a mere passive awareness reaction. We consider far more about our survivability than merely the avoidance of being eaten, though this is a solid cornerstone. Then too, the existence of the first two qualities cited above augments curiosity, and by the qualities of focus and reflection, brings curiosity to a fully conscious and intentional level.

(4) The fourth factor, **imagination** is the most difficult to analyze, but as it is a centerpiece for consciousness, it must be dissected and discussed. First, we might identify imagination as the creative reflection and rearrangement of known things that leads to some unexpected or serendipitous revealing. Sometimes that revealing is in the form of a meaning, and sometimes the

revealing is of arranged pieces that bring new possibilities to light. This last form of imagination – the genesis of possibilities – is vital for our project. Imagination is the grounding for an answer to 'What Can I Do?'

Imagination has often been dubbed the basis for genius, which has the unfortunate affect of suggesting that imagination is a gift for the few. Imagination is not a gift reserved for the few. Imagination emerges from the primal circumstance. This makes imagination a universal human characteristic, not a gift. However, those among us who fully grasp the nature of the primal circumstance as limitless contingency realize freedom as an event only fully expressed through creative imagination. It is here that the genius and the artist come to mind. These individuals are unique only in so far that their ultimate understanding of life as devoid of inherent meaning has driven them to appear extreme, eccentric...or mad. But as the primal circumstance is a universal human condition, imagination is as universal as is the ability to reason and to accumulate and collate experience (i.e., knowledge). A great deal more will be said about imagination below; however, what we might say for now is that even a genius must be in possession of many known things, and in the absence of a store of knowledge there would be nothing on which to exercise his or her imagination and genius.

A point we need to stress here is that these unique human characteristics rest on a very real foundation of the human condition. There is nothing esoteric about these characteristics. Nor is there anything discriminating about them. These qualities are not some spiritual wellspring for some special elite. These qualities are universal throughout humanity. By power of the fact that these are human characteristics they are equally available to us all! That universality needs to be fully understood and kept in mind.

Let me now apply these factors to the Thales circumstance described above.

First, we can say that Thales' rising consciousness convinced him that physical explanations, rather than supernatural explanations, led to an accurate understanding of the world around him. An empirical grasp of the world is a vital step in gaining an accurate material vision. In today's world this is a commonplace understanding, but not in the 5th century, BCE. Therefore, to reveal the true and accurate meaning behind events and things, wresting himself free of an ideology of superstition proved a crucial action for Thales.[40] This was a breakthrough for that time of superstition and magical understanding.

We can say that Thales utilized the power of **reason** as the basis for understanding the world. This facility assembles the raw material we have gathered through our senses and social relations facilitated by what appears to be a human predisposition to logical structuring, which aims at a re-fitting of experience, converting it into a serviceable entity. Reason can be, and ought to be, a creative, fluid process that avoids the rigid idea-systems (ideology) that force prefab answers onto real world issues and events. Reason is the manner in which we form combinations of observed reality. Reason is that part of the human mind that assembles experience into orderly patterns for storage as knowledge.

The second element, **knowledge** is difficult to avoid. We are constantly absorbing experience, re-fitting it, and warehousing it. It is in the nature of the warehousing that the difficulty begins. Knowledge can and often does involve raw information redeployed into useful pattern formations. Raw knowledge is transformed into 'meaning.' However, and unfortunately, we all too often skip over the facility of reason and store knowledge in a prefab structure. The structure of the storehouse represents one of many possible idea-systems we are presented with upon our arrival in this reality. Depending on a prefab ideological structure usually means the jettisoning of any experience that conflict with the ideology. In making the preservation of the ideological structure the predominate goal, much experience and knowledge is cast aside as irrelevant to the needs of the ideological system. The dominate idea-system may actually stand in active opposition to the advancement of both the third and fourth factors that build the intellectual framework, curiosity and imagination.

How and why Thales achieved this critical understanding and reliance on reason is not known, but there can be no doubt that Thales was in possession of the third element: **Curiosity**. We can surmise that Thales overcame the ideological handicaps of his day and with the aid of curiosity – that ultimate enemy of superstition[41] – he uncovered alternatives. It follows that he must have also possessed the tools to accurately observe. We know that Thales must have had a superb educational background[42] that gave him the tools needed to observe. Thales was not just aware, he was conscious of possible alternative explanations for events such as a solar eclipse. The possibility of alternative explanations – alternative explanations made available by the human gift of imagination – was chief among his tools.

The final element of **imagination** is based on the freedom to project into current perceptions of reality all of what we know and have uncovered about certain types of events as they relate to a general reading of our Situation. We then work to combine, recombine, tweak, fiddle and adjust our knowledge of these events in unique and creative ways until a combination either matches up with current perception, or more to our point here, matches up with how things *ought to be*.   To resist the thought of how things ought to be is to resist our fated state of freedom, seen in this case as the freedom to follow curiosity and speculate.

We can certainly speculate that this 'how things ought to be' may in itself be little more than a reflection of our inclination to locate right and wrong within the grace of balance and symmetry. This would be an interesting avenue to explore, but whatever the root cause of the reflection we know that the 'primal circumstance' has condemned us to freedom, and one of the workings of freedom is to circumvent a resignation with how things are, supplanting it with a vision of how things ought to be. This is the chief role of imagination in answering the question 'What Can I Do?'   To visualize how things 'ought' is to struggle toward a precise foundation for this all-consuming question.

As already suggested, it is entirely probable that pattern formation is hardwired into our neural gestalt, causing an inclination toward symmetry and balance. Such an inclination would offer another clue as to why imagination is unique to humanity.   As we all possess a similar neural gestalt, we would then all possess the hardware for this imaginative ability. The science behind this 'hardware' remains for future study. However, the fact remains that a predisposition toward pattern formation and symmetry appears a natural proclivity universal to us all. We must also say that imagination is ultimately (and perhaps ironically) grounded in empirically accumulated knowledge. So, even the brightest among us must possess commonly available knowledge to realize the potential of his or her imaginative gifts. If that empirical knowledge is faulty, our current perceptions (even those visions belonging to a genius) will not properly align with reality. Sometimes this faulty knowledge is due to inadequate tools-at-hand (poor mathematical tools, inadequate sci-entific models, etc.), and sometimes the fault lies with an ideology that dead-ends our vision (it is difficult to prepare for weather if one is possessed of an ideology that claims that the Gods make the wind blow). Whatever the reason, an incorrect or poor vision of reality will lead to a crippled imagination – one lacking sufficient components of ac-curate knowledge – a crippling that can lead us in a fruitless direction.

Raising consciousness revolves around the utilization of all of these factors that combine in humanity to give us our uniqueness – the ability to reason; to accumulating knowledge; to be curious; to be imaginative. All these factors are real, practical, and universal, and all are necessary tools for the advancement of consciousness.

We speak of these four factors as vital to the revealing of *realities*. One of these realities is the direction we must take in answering the question, 'What Can I Do?' These 'realities,' over all, form a web of circumstance or relations that clearly underwrite 'knowing,' but are not empirically obvious. This is especially accurate when considering the realities of power, which are, after all, central to accomplishing anything positive (or negative) in this world. Power is how things get done in this world. Power can be as obvious as a gun, or as hidden as socio-economic influence. Remember always, that with the raising of consciousness we become equipped to understand how things really work in the real world – or don't work in the world. The working out of a real world answer to 'What Can I Do?' involves the use of a 'rising consciousnesses' to fully envelope and reflect on the power relations that exist in the real world. This, in turn, further enhances the raising of consciousness, and so on in the dialectic between human consciousness and real world power relations.

When we use the term real world power relations, many things are brought to mind. Power relations can exist in a family setting, in a neighborhood setting, in business setting, large and small, labor unions, work settings, the city, the nation, the local community. There is literally no end to the environments where power between humans is not worked out. This brings us to the word and concept of 'politics.' For a great many people – perhaps the majority of people – this word, even the mere idea of politics, is disgusting in the extreme. Politics is, as it appears in the public media, a mosh pit, a pig sty, where people without any redeeming qualities struggle in the most immoral and unseemly manner to get their way by heading down a noxious path that is untread by most of us. Speaking quite frankly, this disturbing and cutthroat dog-and-pony show is as distasteful to me as anyone else. Yet I know, and you must know as well, that to really do something about conditions in the real world a political struggle, at some level, is unavoidable.

Politics verses Government.

Politics is the overall process that determines who gets what, how much of it they get, and when do they get it. It should be immediately obvious that this is a process that can quickly lead to pain and very often to violence. Even so, take note, that in witnessing the gallop of suffering across the world's stage we rarely see politics, *per se*. What we *see* is government. Government is the legal, structural expression and the handmaiden of politics. *Seeing* government, rather than politics, accounts for why most activities in the political arena are confusing, difficult to understand, alienating, and pernicious to follow. For clarity, it is best to remember that it is politics, not government, which is the struggle to determine the distribution of the social product as a whole. Government is a structural distortion behind which this fact hides. A moment's reflection will lead you to the necessary conclusion that any answer to the question 'What Can I Do?' will, at bottom, revolve around 'political struggle' rather than government. To blindly plunge into 'governmental answers' is to sap the vitality from the question 'What Can I Do?' and dead-end it. This needs further unpacking.

Government is the mask that refines and disguises this crude struggle for the social product (i.e., the sum total of society's good and services). Government is also the coercive agency by which political decisions on the distribution of the social product are enforced. For the vast majority of us, it is natural to see something in this process if not hostile, then at least beyond our control. Most individuals in any given society can see this picture of alienation as simply an accurate account of the political struggle. The majority of citizens see themselves as remote from government and alienated from the intimacies of decision making. For them, government is a hurtful and malignant entity. For those who benefit from the governmental system of social distribution, the opposite is the case. The more you receive from the political machinations, the more the supporting government appears in a favorable light. For those who acquire the lion's share of social distribution government is seen not just as good and temperate, but as a Capricorn of Beneficence.

For vast segments of the population, the role of government is largely hazy and ill defined. This is no accident. A highly important characteristic of government, at least in part, is to hide the actual nature of the political struggle. The façade of governmental operations conceals the real power relations from us. Exactly how this is perceived depends largely on where the viewer is positioned in relation to both politics and government. As one might suppose, being closer to the decision making process causes the viewer to see the relations as less alien and threatening than for those standing further away. This has to do with proximity to the levers of influence and the powers that can release them. This is most obvious in rigidly defined societies such as found in feudal structures. This is also true of "representative democracies" as the "representatives" determine the distribution of the social product according to the actual political relations (i.e., the socio-economic structural reality that animates and directs the government's distributive goals) and not the constitutional façade that shields it from view. As pure democracy remains only a theoretical entity, it is difficult to gauge the practical consequences to social distribution under such a system.[43]

First, we need to address political knowledge of political relations, and how these relations are typically concealed from us. The concealing is sometimes deliberate manipulation by the power relations themselves. After all, secrecy is a cornerstone of political power. And sometimes the concealing is historically 'deliberate' in the sense that it is a product of inherited ideologies that blind the strugglers as well as the witnesses to the struggle. Both these things make the uncovering and revealing of political relations a far more difficult task and all the more dependent on the above four factors: (1) the ability to reason, (2) accumulating knowledge, and (3) curiosity and (4) the use of imagination.

At times, as the discussion below proceeds, we will need to be forthright, even blunt in our assessment of the power relations we confront in this world. To answer the question 'What Can I Do?' there is no other way. We must confront the nature of power in this world. This bluntness may bring a certain degree of discomfort as it is not often that the power relations which run this world are stripped bare of the legal decorations and ideological trapping that make them palatable. However, it is necessary in order to make clear the way in which consciousness of political relations are made obscure and bring this expanded consciousness within the range or our reaching-out.

Introduction to Politics.

A word about the topic, *political.* When I say 'political' I do not mean the political party you belong to, nor the protest demonstration in which you participated, nor even the act of voting. While all these things are aspects of political relations, and of some importance, 'political' has a wider, more socio-economic meaning that brings us closer to a real understanding of 'politics.'

Defining politics is very simple. As previously stated, politics is the process by which it is decided who gets what, how much of it they get, and when do they get it. The "what" in this case is the total sum of the social product of a given society. For political purposes a society can mean the immediate locale, or it can mean the entire world of humanity, that is, 'society' can range from the very micro, as found in the family and neighborhood, to the very macro, as found in the nation-state and the international arena.

Economically speaking, the distribution of the social product very often means that someone's gain is due to someone else's loss. This is not a pretty picture, but due to the nature of scarcity, an accurate picture. As a consequence, what is taking place in the political process is a fierce and often violent, unrelenting struggle over the social product. The level of ferocity depends on the proximity of two elements. One is the *availability* of the social product, and other is *control* over the social product. Keep these two factors in mind, *availability* and *control,* for they govern the level of coercion and violence present in a particular social order. Government, as detailed above, is both the mask behind which this struggle is carried out and the negotiator that attempts to mediate the ferocity and keep it from spilling over into open bloodshed. Government, while having considerable bearing on the question of 'What Can I Do?' is not the central focus. Our focus is on politics behind the mask and the political acts that are the choices we all make. As we cannot step out of our society we cannot step out of the power relations that are the structural determinates of that society.

As a further elucidation, to say 'political' can mean deciding which restaurant to eat at, or which book to buy, or simply getting up in the morning and going to work. All of these activities represent aspects of distributing the social product. Of course, describing these everyday activities as political sounds strange as you think of some or all of these acts as being trivial, voluntary, and far removed from the pivotal issues of power. The question arises: Are not these, and many other mundane actions, as social-product distribution, completely free of coercion, which is, after all, a central feature of political relations? This is worth considering at some length.

Recognize first that every act, no matter how pedestrian, is locked into the web of social experience and relations in which you live. The matrix of these social relations is ultimately rooted in the relationships of power existent within your society. Let us make this point with an example. The restaurant in which you decide to eat is within your decision-making range principally because of the power of a politically managed economy that widely influences employment, income, advertising, food distribution, mortgage lending, and the business class to which the owner of the restaurant, and you, belong, etc. Even this seemingly prosaic action is interwoven with many of the social and economic elements within which you live and choose. Without being aware of it, a system of subtle force guides you through the decision making of events that are seemingly trivial actions.

The fact that we do not ordinarily consider these activities as pressed by power relations is testimonial to the pervasiveness of inherited ideologies that obscure and misdirect much of our thinking. Ideology and doctrine are the premier ways in which we are turned away from acknowledging the power relations at work to influence even apparently random decisions. With very little exception, every act has some implication for this web of power relations. It is also true that seeing the extent of this system may be beyond our prevailing consciousness. You, and I, as distasteful as it is to contemplate, are creatures, (but not marionettes!) of political forces of which we are typically unaware. Part of the individual task in the individual revelation of 'What Can I Do?' is to draw back the veil to allow for the *seeing* of the reality of these power relations. We call this *raising political consciousness*.

By dint of ideology, political relations blend into the social matrix in such a way as to misdirect an accurate view of the power arrangements and cause the coercive factors to appear normal and fitting, that is, make coercion appear *a-political*. As mentioned, this misdirection represents the transforming power of the prevailing system of ideas (ideology). In the most general sense, all of my *social* relations (e.g., who I choose to marry, where I plan to live, who I choose to befriend, etc.) can be looked at as an expression of historically determined *power* relations. Where I stand in the social system, that is, the power I automatically wield as a member of a certain socio-economic class was historically determined. This social positioning has the overriding influence on my life's chances and direction. Can this Situation be changed – yes, definitely it can, but only by exercising a force and focus so one dimensional and exclusive that all other considerations go by the way-side.

Living within any social system means that from the moment of my birth I have breathed in the ideological atmosphere, the idea-system of my time, making all that I witness seem as normal as the hands at the end of my arms. Where I am born, into what time in history, into what class, what race, has profound implications for me and the idea-systems that influence and direct my thinking. I am consciously aware of power relations in actions overtly related to the governing structure of our society – elections, party affiliation, taxes collection, police activity, and so on – but all of my other acts, no matter how trivial, and most of my thinking, have elements of power relations about them and are also political, only I am not completely conscious of them. It is actually more accurate to say that I am politically unconscious. All this seems very tedious and although we may understand it, we would prefer not to dwell on such matters. Many times we actually prefer unconsciousness to political consciousness. This represents a serious impediment to the raising of consciousness and stands in the way of any authentic answer to the question: 'What Can I Do?'

Political Consciousness.

In a previous section we explored general consciousness. The task now before us is to explore political consciousness. What this entails is to detail consciousness as it confronts political power. As it is political power that is the vehicle for actual social movement and change, both positive and negative, this will bring us more fully in line with an answer to the question, 'What Can I Do?'

Political consciousness, perhaps more pointedly than consciousness in general, is engendered by the 'curiosity syndrome,' that derivative of our instinct for survival and well-being. Survival often depends on asking the right questions. Beyond the reflex for survival, political consciousness begins its actualization along similar lines as general consciousness, that is, a reaching out to engage. It utilizes the tool of focus to envelope specific things, and draws them back in for willful (which is to say intentional) reflection. There are, however, levels and degrees, and the objective of political consciousness is stated as specific in regard to this or that impacting event. In other words, political consciousness has a discriminating intention that sets it apart from general consciousness. The animation of political consciousness is the survival instinct as felt through the unease we all feel when considering the coercive nature of the political apparatus (i.e., government). The intention of political consciousness is curiosity about that power apparatus and its impact on our daily lives.

This curiosity is not welcomed by certain elements within the power structure. Recall that political consciousness is a reaching out to willfully engage the power relations found in a specific social order. Again, due to certain economic rules underwriting politics – *viz.*, the way in which the social product is distributed being almost universally unequal – this tends to be the focal point of both power relations and those curious about it. So while this reaching-out-to-engage is not a hostile act, *per se*, it will be unwelcome by many within the power structure. Remember, that the political process is a struggle where someone gains and someone loses. For "the someone" who gains, close scrutiny is never welcome as it always carries the threat of exposure and some fear of reprisals. Therefore, in reaching-out-to-engage one must be prepared for some probable defensive maneuvering on the part of the power structure, from pooh-poohing the attempt, to outright condemnation, even to a violent suppressive reaction.

To more fully appreciate this reaching-out-to-engage let us look into a most basic level of political consciousness, which is not a true political consciousness at all but a reaction we will call political *awareness*. We are using 'awareness' in the same sense as outlined in the above discussion of general consciousness, that is, awareness as a manifestation of a more one-dimensional instinct for survival and well-being. Therefore, 'political awareness' is an awareness of power that lacks the fully conscious grasp of power relations. The force of power acting upon the individual arouses this awareness. The individual response to awareness is necessarily vague. This bears some elaboration. First, a few preparatory remarks.

In some form or another all societies cohere in the way that they do because of the specific arrangements of power within that society. For the solitary individual, the social pressures that guide daily decisions and movements are located within the power relations manifested by the social structure. This is a basic understanding that cannot be avoided in any study of the social process.

The power relations are almost always veiled. However, the veil can be drawn back. This uncovering of power relations is the first step in raising political consciousness. The uncovering leads to the revealing of specific meanings derived from the observed power relations. As the power structure gives up its secrets, the ideological facade will fall away and the revealed relations will lose their mystery. Once the aura of mystery disappears, further revealing will lead to the power relations being stripped of much of their revered legitimacy, thus undermining the political authority necessary for day-to-day governmental operation.[44]

How, specifically, is this to be accomplished? Following the four abilities of reason, knowledge, curiosity and imagination the veil can be stripped away and any ideological misdirection corrected. Reason and the absorption of experience is a natural ability to us all. However, there are certain choices to be made regarding the 'truth' engendered by a reasoning process set to reveal the meaning of raw experience. It is entirely possible to choose to see the world as real and material, but this type of seeing is in no way a universal understanding of how the world works. Simply put, we can choose a material interpretation of the world and how it works, or we can choose an ethereal or a transcendental perspective on how the world works. And between these two broad perspectives, the material and the transcendental, there is a meridian of sub systems. Thus seeing 'truth' is not a natural ability, but it is a choice[xxiii]. The question then becomes: What is available in the world of power relations to help us make this choice on truth?

The first question to ask is 'do we depend on a pre-existing idea structure to reveal meaning behind experience?' If so, then we are, after a fashion, depending on someone else's choice for the truth. This may be a 'truth' engineered by a small group, as in propaganda doctrine issued through a national state, or this 'truth' may be historically driven, as are most circumstances involving such ideological considerations as racism and xenophobia. The historically driven is the most encompassing and the most tenacious, and is a vital clue in making the choice. A pre-existing idea-system was designed by history for a reason, though this is not likely the reason of individuals, but rather the 'cunning of history.' So ask, what is the reason behind the idea structure and to what ends does it lead? More pointedly, given the nature of a particular power structure, it is best to ask: Who wins by this idea-system, and who loses?

Such a question can be asked of nearly all ideologies, but let us take racism as a pre-existing idea-system and unveil it for analysis. Reason and knowledge will immediately tell us that there is no scientific basis for race and therefore race is a mask behind which other forces

---

[xxiii] This claim was explained in a lengthy discussion detailed in the above chapter, "Truth." P. 27

are struggling for dominance. If we reach out with curiosity and engage extreme historical examples of racism (e.g., the US and South Africa) many things become revealed. Through reason we can quickly deduce that the forces are struggling over the control and distribution of the social product. No surprises here. What lies behind the ideology of the many forms of racism is an unequal control and distribution of the social product. Racism is a veil behind which that reality of imbalance is hidden. Next we can use imagination to ask what the end of this ideology is; to where does this idea structure lead? By creatively rearranging the pieces provided by history, we can project that there is no good end to which racism can lead, and certainly no peaceful end. Reason has been our guide. Curiosity has been our engagement. Our knowledge of history has been the provider of the pieces in play. And imagination has rearranged these pieces to reveal the ends. Now one is in a much better position to make a judgment regarding the 'truth' of this ideology of racism, and more than that, to make a choice of rather or not to follow this version of the 'truth.' If any one of these pieces is missing (the most likely missing piece would be 'knowledge') then the choices rest on an inaccurate grasp of the Situation and will lead to shaky results.

The above was a quick example, but we can do this with all ideologies, and come to realize that not all ideologies are distasteful and lead to bad ends. A little reflection on the ideology of science will reveal this. The results of a scientific idea-system can be turned to unsavory ends, but as a system itself it is difficult to see where scientific ideology is partial to one social group over another. The ideology of science can be turned to the struggle for dominance, but unlike racism, is not inherently predisposed to power and oppression. Unless negative political forces intervene, the ends of scientific ideology will typically funnel into such results as increased food production, curbing epidemics, medical advancement, renewable energy, etc. By grasping the locus of ideology, you are in a much better position to judge and choose 'truth.'

As suggested above, a drawing back of the ideological veil will damage political doctrine causing a great loss of legitimacy and authority. In stating this, the claim is brought forward that much political 'authority' is granted by a sense of *reverence* promoted by an ideology that misdirects the material view by substituting the abstract symbols of government for the facts of politics. This is to say, that much government legitimacy and authority is actualized through reverence for key esoteric principles (e.g., patriotism, sanctity of law, nationalism, racial purity, etc.) and not the hard facts surrounding political struggle. A grasp of this sense of 'reverence' serves to illustrate the difference between political awareness and political consciousness. Reverence veils the power relations behind abstract principles leaving one with only a vague sense of the forces at work without any clear grasp of their true origin and purpose. We might say that I am 'aware' of the forces at work around me in my society, but I fail to fully perceive their meaning and their true impact on me. Consequently, awareness, as opposed to consciousness, tends to 'feel' the threat of political power rather than grasp and unfold it for a comprehensive viewing. Awareness is to be stuck squinting at political authority through some ideological lens of legitimacy, with the actual material working of the power relations behind the legitimacy as wholly misunderstood or veiled and out of 'sight.' This is true even of so-called entitlement programs. Is public education for enlightened or indoctrination? Are social safety nets to protect the population or to minimize social friction? As *noblesse oblige* has a definite agenda, the answers often lie hidden in the nature of the politics veiled behind government, and not government itself.

To clarify: In the case of 'political awareness' the individual is only passively aware of power relations. I can get a parking ticket, enroll my child in public school, be inducted into the military, or receive food stamps, and all this can happen to me without my possessing any precise knowledge of the power arrangements at work to guide these events. I am aware only that something is happening to me. Like Josef K,[xxiv] I am compelled to move here and there without understanding the exact reasons compelling the move. Drawing on the example offered in a previous section, the deer is aware of the wolves in the same way that I am aware of being acted upon by forces outside of myself. Like the deer, I move, almost instinctually, re-sponding to an unseen threat, but understand very little of those forces making up the threat. I am *passively aware* of the power in the vicinity and have only a vague notion of the nature of the power behind the threat. I move about, not fully in conscious control of my own movements. This is something I sense rather than know.

[xxiv] Josef K, the central character in Franz Kafka's 1924 novel, *The Trial*, where K is inexplicably shuffled about by events and persons, the actions of which are never fully explained either to K or the reader.

This pawn like absence of active engagement is symptomatic of simple political awareness and is the lowest rung of political sensitivity. Getting stuck at this low level of political awareness will mire the individual in feelings of alienation, confusion, powerlessness, and in the face of the forces surrounding him, often leave the hapless individual wandering about the daily routine in a fog or daze. This state of confusion and helplessness is decidedly to the advantage of the powers that control the social structure and is often deliberately fostered. In representative democracies, we can see this fostering of confusion most obviously when witnessing campaign strategy for election to public office. An important point here is that the fog and misdirection are not the goal, *per se*, but simply endemic to the process, thus fully illustrating the insidiousness of an alienating ideology.

In keeping with the defining characteristics of general consciousness, achieving political consciousness, together with feelings of empowerment, is an active, engagement. At the risk of pointing out the unmistakable, to engage requires facilities of engagement. The discussion now revolves around the questions: (1) What is the nature of these faculties of engagement that facilitate political consciousness; (2) and from where do these faculties come?

Faculties of engagement.

Passive awareness requires only inactive reception. This is not to suggest that passivity is a kind of dullness, but rather a level of alertness that lacks intentional curiosity. The opposite of this is a reaching out. Every form of intentional reaching-out must abandon inactivity and proceed actively. This is greatly facilitated by offering a free and fearless reign to curiosity.

While it is true that reaching out to engage springs from the curiosity syndrome, engagement itself must possess the power of dynamic action. This is a way of saying that for me to reach out, I must possess the systematic tools to do so. Besides the obvious – that is, my central nervous system – what is the nature these tools and what would make them available? To reveal the nature of these tools of engagement let me offer a rather simple illustration.

I sit at my desk and I look over at the far corner of the desktop. I see a coin. The coin looks elliptical. From where I sit I am only *aware* that the coin appears elliptical. This is different from knowing, for I *know* the coin is not elliptical. In spite of how the coin appears to me from where I *passively* 'see,' I *actively* know that the coin is round. Let us examine what has occurred. I glance at a coin and what I *see* (passive) and what I *know* (active) clash. I sense that something is not quite right with what I see, something is 'off' with passive awareness. I am bothered about what has happened to my 'looking.' The passivity is dissatisfying and becomes a source of unease. The unease arouses my curiosity as a way to resolve the tension between my 'looking' and my 'knowing'. I now reached out to the coin with curiosity about what I see. I focus, that is, I reach out to actively envelop the coin. Next, with active intent, I draw the vision of the coin back for an engagement with active reflection against my previously warehoused *knowledge* of coins and looking. Through *reflecting* the meaning of what I was seeing is revealed. I am now conscious that something called 'perspective' caused the coin to appear elliptical. The chief dynamic tool that I used to actively engage and realign appearance with material reality was my warehoused knowledge about coins *and* about perspective. The dynamic nature of the enveloping tool is focused curiosity. The reflection of the engaged entity (in this case a coin) against previous knowledge is the source by which meaning is revealed. This is a very simple example. Yet even for more complicated or exotic issues the dynamic nature of the engaging tools remains the same; the tools are a curiosity about what makes me uneasy and knowledgeable of the real, material world. Curiosity is the front-runner, turning the passive into the active. Without these dynamic tools awareness never reaches the level of consciousness.

Also consider two things: First, as we have previously discussed, curiosity ultimately springs from the instinct to survive and be well, and is universal throughout our species, and two, knowledge, while the capacity for which is a natural human ability, is itself not a given. Knowledge is not universal to humanity. Knowledge about the real and practical world must be extensively cultivated. In the absence of knowledge, curiosity has no place to go to relieve the tension provoked by a passive looking. Only knowledge can give curiosity an extended direction. Let us see how this would work in a not so simple illustration.

Through news sources I become aware of droughts in central Russia, desertification in Mexico, hurricanes in the Caribbean and monsoon flooding in Asia, all massive and unseasonable changes in the environment. I do not have to be personally present in the areas of drought or flooding, to understand that the strength and their unusual appearance may have some connection with climate change. This can, and probably will make me uneasy, even if only vaguely. It may be reported that some of these events are geographically close, or I have been persuaded by the reports that some of the events precipitate certain economic effects which will affect my well-being. It is a perfectly natural reaction to feel a sense of unease with an undertow of curiosity. I feel compelled to reach out and engage the events. I may even grasp what seems to me to be the most relevant and threatening of the events and draw it toward me, but here I might be stopped. Without the web of knowledge to summon up meaning to the event I am left helpless and frustrated. In the end, without a storehouse of knowledge concerning climate change, weather patterns, some sense of geologic history, I must dismiss the events as something about which I can do nothing. This can be an intimidating and alienating experience.

Along with distinguishing political consciousness from political awareness, the factors of focused curiosity and knowledge not only allow us too actively and effectively engage with our environment – in this case, our political environment – they tend to replace, not just the confusion, but also the feelings of helplessness and that drifting sense of powerlessness. It is also true that with knowledge comes the energy of anger. This is a natural human reaction. Threats are very real and they provoke anger. But only knowledge offers direction for the energy of anger. Through knowledge, my frustration and anger can be directed and pointed. Through knowledge, I can begin to find myself centered with a growing sense of control rather than being controlled. With knowledge, I can more fully anchor myself in the real world and give direction to my efforts at 'What Can I Do?'

Raising *political* consciousness.

The first thing to note about political consciousness, and in particular the *raising* of political consciousness, is that this is an action on your part that will take place in a hostile atmosphere. Your allies will be few, your opponents numerous. And your most damning obstacle is the prevailing ideology, that idea-system that history has conjured to support and maintain some existing status quo. It is the most damning because its very ubiquitous quality allows this ideology to hide in plain sight, with the vast majority of individuals adopting its precepts without thought or question. Ideology is a major source of political *unconsciousness*. But ideology is not the only obstacle. The powerful living actors in the socio-economic environment are the other obstacle. These actors include those who direct information flow as organizers of the mass media, those who direct the distribution of the social product as the controllers of the governing apparatus, and those who both receive and distribute the social product; these actors would include the captains of industry, investors of capital, moguls of mass media, elected representatives, *et al.* It is a rare individual, or group of individuals, who could be found sitting in these, the highest seats of power, and at the same time show any interest in a growth of political consciousness within the social order. Political consciousness is one of the few authentic threats to any power structure. Remembering that ignorance is a form of secrecy, and secrecy is a major source of control, and therefore power, it is easy to see why promoting extensive education is hardly in the interests of a ruling elite. To provide a sub-standard education, or better yet little or no education at all for the general population, is a positive consideration for any governing elite. This is not to suggest that promoting ignorance is deliberate, or even a necessarily conscious goal. Ideology can blind the ruling elite and cause that elite to mouth ideological sentiments that rationalize the damage they do. Often, they come to believe the myths, platitudes and outright canards themselves. This is the insidious controlling power of ideology. We cannot step outside to view and analyze an ideology from within that ideology. To overcome the power of one ideology we must employ a different ideology, a counter-ideology, if you will. We can see the effect of this counter-ideology by reviewing the overcoming of an ideology of superstition with an ideology of science.

Reflect, too, on effects of ignorance upon your existential condition. Lack of developed knowledge exacerbates a mood of helplessness and alienation. It is therefore in the interests of the power structure to frustrate not just the free flow of information and knowledge, but also the acquiring of the tools to organize this information. The rigidity, ruthlessness and absoluteness of a political structure's governing apparatus vary only by degree, and therefore the hostility to knowledge varies only by degree. This is not a hopeless situation for the raising of consciousness. Knowledge, by its very nature is universally available, and therefore 'knowing' is always possible, even in the harshest of political environments. However, an inhospitable environment makes the achievement of political consciousness a true uphill battle. The question is how to take that first step.

To answer this, let me return to the example of the Greek philosopher, Thales, we offered in a section above. Thales lived in a time where the real nature of material events was often shrouded in mystery. The chief ideological formations were variations of superstition. This bears a certain resemblance to the fog surrounding politics. Political institutions are typically shrouded in the transcendentalism of patriotism, destiny, and classism, all lost in the superstitious fanaticism of such as racial superiority, or divine purpose, then wrapped up in the gilded reverence offered by a legal system that spearheads the ideology. The real workings of power relations are largely unknown to the population at-large, and even, we might add, to the key players as well. Like Thales before us, we must come to the realization that something solid and material is going on here. We cannot raise political consciousness unless we realize that the chauvinism of the state has a purpose. The political state, in the form of government, has an historical design that is not meant for any overt unveiling. Ideology stands in the way of raising consciousness. It is here that simple political *awareness* serves its best purpose.

What we think is happening is very probably happening.
Like in the illustration of the deer used above, we humans also possess survival instincts, instincts that support an alert system we have been referring to as awareness. Recognize that awareness, political or other-

wise, is an opportunity. Awareness is a trigger for curiosity and therefore consciousness. How often have I heard my neighbor grumble about taxes, or those damn fools who keep plunging the country into wasteful wars and painful depressions, or grouse over the rich bastards that have everything while everyone else just 'gets by.' This complaining is an alert system. It is political awareness at work. It is a political awareness that I share with my neighbor. We are not imagining things, my neighbor and I – I am not imagining things. We are as the deer that knows wolves are in the area, and we are alerted. We need only to trust ourselves, that is, trust our own instinct for survival through awareness: *What we think is happening is very probably happening*. However, unlike the deer, we humans can ignore this alert, this awareness, look away, and pretend that nothing is happening, erect a wall of rationalizations between us and the awareness, but we do so at our own peril. However, at this point, we become the willing prey for the wolves, even their accomplice in our own destruction.

Consider some doctrinaire claims. Taxes are my patriotic duty. I must sacrifice for the greater good of the nation. Our leaders are wiser than I. The rich have worked hard and are deserving of their wealth, etc. These are common political canards in our modern world, yet often these claims come with an uneasy feeling. We have a sense that something is amiss, that things are out of alignment. This *gut feeling* is that something is not quite right with some or all of these claims. This gut feeling is my alert system at work. Like the deer, our first step is to trust the gut feelings, that is, trust our survival instincts. The deer is an intimate of the terrain and knows the manner in which a twig snaps, or a stalk of grass bows. Our senses tell us when certain events are not congruent with the landscape. Like the deer, we are an integrated component of the political terrain, for we have always existed within an environment of power relations. We can surely sense or feel when events around us do not properly line up, a word slip, body language, a mix of events, all can trigger our awareness. When events feel out of place, unbalanced, we feel out of place. These feelings will prepare us to reach out to the context or event with the best tools we find available.

First, we must judge the best direction to reach out. Here, we separate and distinguish ourselves from the deer. Our instincts will prove inadequate to proceed beyond gut feelings and awareness. Unlike the position of the deer, the wolves in *our* lives are *not* operating solely on instinct. These wolves are highly skilled and have developed habits based on a cunning manipulation not only of their environment of power relations, but of knowledge concerning the context in which they hunt – that is, knowledge of us and the social landscape in which to find us. There is always the ultimate danger that the wolf is more conscious than the deer.[xxv]

The terrain in which both the wolf and the deer inhabit is the social and political landscape in which history has placed the adversaries. To elevate my consciousness, I must learn the social and political skills of the wolf. This

---

[xxv] Much of the advice of Machiavelli to "The Prince" is based in the supposition that the prince ought to be more 'conscious' than his subjects.

learning is fashioned by the nature of the manipulation and knowledge of the political landscape. If I fail to learn the social and political skills of the wolf I will be their accomplice, their willing quarry. If I do not come to understand the terrain I will not survive. I will be devoured.

Raising my political consciousness means a more careful study of the power relation in which I live. It is vital to understand that I, myself, will be initially resistant to this kind of reflection. This is a natural reaction. I am not lazy, or stupid, but alienated. ("Who cares, and anyway there is nothing anyone can do about it!") Rather than being stupid, lazy or uninterested, I am overcome by an apathy that has its roots sunk deep in feelings of powerlessness and alienation. I am literally overwhelmed by the context of my Situation. These are difficult feelings to overcome, but I must overcome them as they serve to promote only resignation and a greater sense of helplessness, all this spiraling my consciousness downward.

Keep in mind that one of the intents of power is to promote these feeling of alienation and apathy. Although it is tempting to conclude that this is a deliberate scheme on the part of the agents of power, it is not necessarily a conscious process, but a corollary adjunct of the dominate socio-political ideology. This dominate ideology can program this alienation into the social and political landscape through an historically conditioned legal framework that causes change to be so time-consuming, arduous, expensive, or even dangerous, that frustration leads to a desire to slink away and sink into the cave of unconsciousness. After all, to be unconscious shields me from my own powerlessness.

To desire unconsciousness is a natural reaction to the pain of alienation.

A lack of consciousness is a mark of a highly successful ideology, in that it not only inculcates a mood of helplessness in the general population, but to also blinds that population to the source of these feelings. To blind the population to the nature of the power structure is a heady accomplishment for any ideology. It must again be noted that in the case of ideology, this is not necessarily a conscious conspiracy of the agents of power, but more the conspiracy of historical forces that serve their interests. Recall that ideology is a system of ideas that is developed by historically engineered problems which exist dynamically in dialogue with human attempts to solve them. However, to *exploit* the existing ideology can well be a conspiracy of agents of power.

To cause the population to *want to be politically blind* is an ultimate achievement for any power structure. It is easy to judge the effectiveness and power of the political hierarchy by how much the populace wants to avoid political involvement. In the United States, for example, nearly half of the voting population refuses, on a steady basis, to participate in the electoral process. Such a level of apathy is a huge victory for a political legitimacy that actually thrives in the midst of paradox: A material inequality of historic proportions supporting a doctrine of equality and shared power. Instead of this contradiction leading to a crisis of rationality, it leads to misdirection, anomie, and passivity; overt oppression is largely unnecessary.[45] This achievement is explicable only by a solid grasp on the power of ideology. Additionally, the fact that this non-event of non-participation is rarely mentioned in the media and even more rarely analyzed is testimonial to that ideological power hiding in plain sight. Such alienation is an ideological promotion and is the earmark of a highly successful power structure. The deer have resigned themselves to their fate. In a phrase, they have surrendered the political terrain.

The terrain is the world in which we live. More specific to our point, the political terrain in which we find ourselves is the system of power relations that does not merely surround us, but is a system into which we are fully integrated. The wolf and the deer live cheek to jowl, in a manner of speaking, i.e., they live in a shared ideological environment. It is this landscape of power relations that we must uncover and reveal in order to acquire the tools to reach out and fully grasp the things and events that manipulate and control our lives. We must realize that the totality of the circumstance in which we find ourselves is *real*, not fantasy, not metaphysical, not surreal. This means that we must first suspect that the tools we were given, that is, suspect that our inherited idea-system is part of the trap. We must therefore begin with an examination of ourselves. We must uncover the ideology that compels us, explains the world for us, drives us; we must examine the nature of the ideology that organizes our vision of the reality. This uncovering of 'ourselves,' – the consciousness that defines us – is a first step in the process we call the raising of political consciousness, a raising that makes possible a meaningful answer to the question 'What Can I Do?'

We must also realize that the real, concrete terrain into which we are integrated is different for everyone. No two individuals stand in the same place in this terrain at the same time. Thus, no two Situations are precisely the same. Nor are they in the grip of exactly the same idea-system or share the same view of the landscape. So, as I am different from you, my consciousness will be different from yours. This fact alone, the different placement and resulting consciousness of individuals, goes a long way toward accounting for the vociferous disagreements between individuals as to the issues our society faces. This seems obvious, but it often goes unrecognized, which exacerbates much unnecessary frustration. The problem may not be some hand-me-down ideology, but simply how our position in the terrain excites one idea-system as opposed to another. This is a way of saying that my position in the socio-historical landscape encourages an idea-system that defines my individual consciousness – that is, defines me. It seems to follow that changing our placement in the landscape affects our consciousness, changes who we are, with significant consequences for our Situation. This is an important notion that will be explored a bit later.

Although we humans may share many aspects of consciousness, no one will need to uncover and reveal the exact same features of the terrain to raise individual political consciousness. To a certain extent this streamlines the process. To be effective, every uncovering experience need only be appropriate to an individual's position in the social matrix, rather that position is shared with others or not shared. Ultimately, the unveiling is an individual process of self-revelation. This specified uncovering and revelation will bring a change to who I am and therefore greatly effect my position in the landscape and offer me alternatives in where I need to go to answer the question 'What Can I Do?' In this most general sense, political consciousness raising, even mass consciousness raising, can be best understood as an individual process, a Situational action that, by definition of the Situation, is a process ultimately connected with humanity as a whole.

Understanding political consciousness through understanding who you are.

Who am I? This is perhaps the most penetrating and universal question one can ask to launch the search for individual political consciousness. The question, 'Who am I?' connects the personal world with the objective world, which in the case of this project is the power relations that work diligently to *prevent* authentic self-realization, to deny the individual the freedom necessary for self-definition, and deny universal connection. [xxvi] Just the contrary is the case; the power relations work in such a way as to define individuals within a social order, and we must add, define them in a way that does not typically serve their best interests. [46] This can be said regardless of your position in the social structure. Those near the top of the social hierarchy may also be used by social forces against their best interests. The forces of history, in the form of ideology, often hit hardest at the top. The elite near the pinnacle of the social order are often so damned by a slavish devotion to the demands of their station that the core essence of their freedom was shunted from their view and sealed off from them long ago. Their Situational ethics,

---

[xxvi] To refresh on the universal human connection, see the above section, *Choice, Responsibility, and Connectedness.* P. 77

even their very grasp on their existential Being, may be so utterly compromised as to obfuscate their common, universal human self-image. The loss of this common sense of humanity would go a long way to satisfy questions surrounding much of the unconscionable Machiavellian behavior we witness. And ideology has enabled much of this to be politically unconscious behavior.

Searching for an answer to the question of who you are greatly increases the possibility of developing a deeper consciousness of both the inner and outer worlds. A choice now looms ahead for us, a choice for all humanity. We can either choose a truth about ourselves or passively allow the historically driven, power relations in the world to choose that truth for us, which is to say ideologically define us in a way that suits the best interests of those relations found at the helm of the power structure[xxvii].

The more passive is your engagement with the brute fact of your existence – at least as it is integrated within this power-relation landscape – the more likely will you act out a cruel political discrepancy between authenticity and alienation. If you let it happen, your *passive* interface with the power relations that work to define you will cause you to become a creature *actively* living for the interests of other forces, those social forces that define the 'truth' of power relations. Your self-definition will then become an alien-you devouring the authentic-you from inside your very own consciousness.

[xxvii] Keep in mind that the 'helm of the power structure' is a dialogue between those who occupy the seats of power and the historical forces they confront. Despite appearances, these individuals are not completely in control of either events or the ideological factors in play. They often describe themselves as pawns of events rather than kings.

Remaining passive vis-à-vis the power relations dominate in worldly society will encourage us to be defined completely and act as a collaborator in our own exploitation. This seems strange. This seems the opposite of what one would expect. One would expect (and hope) that passivity would result in being left alone. Unfortunately, for the reluctant and the passive, such abandonment of active choice will not result in avoidance of the power relations of your society. Passivity will cause us to become a means to an end, an instrument of malicious forces that are either indifferent or openly hostile to the survival and well-being of an authentic humanity.

In specific terms, this is what is meant: To be exploited means that our survival needs become *necessarily* secondary to others in a social order that exists in a total mode of wide disparity in the distribution of the social product. This is a fancy way of saying that one person's gain is another's loss, with the losers being the exploited. The material evidence is ubiquitous. Witness how the wealth of stockholders in health insurance companies grow in inverse proportion to the health and well-being of the insured. Or see when private developers exploit the legal right of imminent domain to seize individual homes and farms for the enhancement of those same private developers. Or understand when mass unemployment generates downward pressure on wages that reaps huge rewards for the owners of the means of production and distribution. These illustrations represent distribution of the social product that is in the favor of certain groups over other groups. Of course, it must be noted that while all these actions seem somehow wrong – that is, a blush of that sense of 'imbalance' and 'vulnerability' described in the first section – there are transformational rationalizations at work to fit the imbalance into an existing ideology, an idea-system that makes what we 'instinctively' know to be wrong, 'ideologically' right; e.g., it's all due to the 'invisible hand' of the marketplace, and thus our sense of powerlessness and alienation is heightened and reinforced. The ideological fix is in.

Even so, ideological rationalization is not the immediate point here. The point is that a passive political response in the face of the kind of vulnerability inherent in grossly unequal material distribution will not just be ultimately contradictory to the survival of the social order, but personally disastrous for the survival of the many human beings in that social order. Even more to the point of this project: On an existential level a failure of political consciousness in the face of these hostile forces will also cause a loss of a true sense of self. It is clear that survival and the lose of self are of obvious importance, and related, but this last – the loss of self – has received less attention and is more in line with the purpose of this study. The securing of the self is vital to raising consciousness. To gain an accurate understand of this must be treated in practical terms.

In the earlier section on general consciousness, we suggested that consciousness was a bit like describing who you are, or somewhat oddly, how you are. Locating, uncovering, and revealing an answer to 'who are you?' is a giant step. This giant step will locate your existential position in your world. Your position will be both individual and communal. No one can stand in your unique spot in the landscape, yet you will share much of this, your Situation, with others.

Knowledge of your unique position will put you in a place to actively reach out, engage and envelope the things in your world. To raise your consciousness, that is, to make the most of this engagement, you will need to develop the relevant tools to reach out into the world, to connect with the facticity around you.

First and above all else, you must first come to see yourself as rooted in this real world of power relations. This is uppermost, and you cannot proceed without this primary realization. Following that, and to restate the tools already listed above, you must understand fully that you already have not only the ability to reason, but the responsibility to do so. Be unafraid of curiosity. Work to accumulate a storehouse of experience and knowledge. And understand that imagination is a universal human capability and can be developed to a very high degree.

The power of all these elements is grounded in an accumulated experience shaped by reflection and integrated into a general web of knowledge. Coupled with the first derivative of that instinct to survive, (i.e., curiosity), knowledge is the central element to the process of the raising of general consciousness. With your need to survive always running in the background, knowledge of power relations is the key to the process of raising a political consciousness necessary for you to answer the question, 'What Can I Do?'

We have said that knowledge is the basic tool, but the tool is not the 'process.' Make no mistake about the raising of consciousness. It is a process, and not an easy one. The effort that goes into the raising of consciousness consumes both time and energy, and both in great amounts. Who you are – your existential position is a complex issue. You can start by understanding that as a human being you are social, historical and ontological. This last – the 'ontological you' – has far reaching implications in terms of your extended sense of reality. However, for the sake of space, and immediate relevance in answering the basic practical questions concerning power relations, we must set ontology aside.[47] It is enough to say that at some point, ontology, as a treatment of your Being, must be looked into in detail to further your understanding of the self and its relationship to all dimensions of reality. You will find this 'search' both personally fulfilling and intellectually rewarding.[48]

As we will bypass the more overt ontological issues when asking the question, who are you, the question will consequently be limited in two ways. First, we will restrict 'the You' with a defining reference to the immediate issues confronting you. And second, the consequence of the first restriction requires that who you are right now, (i.e., confronting immediate Situations) is seen and understood as all the outcomes of Situations you have faced historically. In other words, who you are *existentially* (your immediate position in the landscape of time and space) is a position that is an understandable development traceable to that which you are *historically* (your presence in accordance with past actions, both individual and historical). Together, this dialectical configuration – the immediate you in dialogue with the historical you – reveals for all *who* you are socially and politically, which is another way of saying *how* you are integrated into the terrain which both defines and responds to your re-defining engagement. One sense of this relationship is that the raising of your political consciousness is a consequence of immediate activity that will develop a new historical you. Demonstrating how this development of a 'new you' can happen is the next task. This is a real and practical problem, so a practical sketch is in order.

Raising Political Consciousness as a Practical Process.

Illustrations are in order: You are a junior attending the University of California at Los Angeles. You don't dwell on it very much, but in the back of your mind you are aware that your family is well off and you live both a comfortable and stable life. You sit in an air-conditioned classroom and idly listen to a lecture on English medieval literature. This may be interesting, or perhaps not, but ultimately it bears some connection to the landscape and context in which you find yourself. This awareness is hazy on your part, and equally hazy is the thought that English literature does not seem of immediate relevance to the sleazy politics and ugly images that are beginning to assault you in this world in which you live. You are chagrined to discover that much of the immediate relevance of your studies appear minor or absent altogether. Overall, your studies seem to lack any sense of pertinence (a common complaint with university students everywhere and at all times). This makes your study of literature vaguely boring and you uneasy and frustrated. But as a student you are in a uniquely opportune Situation to tackle these issues.

So you are touched by a world out of kilter and mired in suffering and injustice. For reasons not fully understood by you, this worldview deeply affects you and your feeling for life and especially the meaning and relevancy of your own life. The calluses of cynicism that block the light from your distressed spirit is yet to form. Of great importance is the fact that you are still able to ask a deeply troubling, personal question: What can I do about all this horror and ugliness? This is a vital question, and as long as you are able to ask it you have a hand and a foot inside political consciousness. As you have not yet been made indifferent by incessant exposure, you ache for an answer to this question so affecting the vision of your life. The 'I' in this question being the critical turning point. Revealing an answer to 'What Can I Do?' will change who you are, just as changing who you are will reveal an answer to 'What Can I Do?'

As you view the world, you wonder at the sympathy you feel for the downtrodden, or perhaps it is empathy, or perhaps you sense their pain is somehow a direct but ill-formed personal threat? Consider that any of these feelings are awareness 'alerts' and any one of them can turn 'awareness' into the 'curiosity syndrome.' This is a positive turning-on. It draws you into a living equation with the objective world around you. In many ways, your effort is less demanding than those tasks hounding your work-a-day contemporaries, your contemporaries that find themselves frozen in a jungle of economic survival and have neither the time nor the energy to contemplate the disgust they often feel with the state of their world. As I said, as a student you are in the perfect spot. [xxviii] Your lack of integration into the socio-economic order has given you a freedom to search only for relevance.

The *relevant* answer to your search is as easily defined as it is demanding. For example, the range of the troubles you see is too large to swallow at one sitting. Instead, you must pick an issue, but not an issue at random. Be selfish and select an issue that is for you *personally* particularly irksome, *your* relevant issue that plays on *your* mind. The relevance of this issue might be vague and disintegrated, which is not a bad thing. The vagueness of the relevance is symptomatic of the awareness level rather than the consciousness level. It is an awareness of something menacing. It matters less what the issue is than that it seems to you very *personal*. Personal is always relevant. Pick an action or a thing that truly gets under your skin because it strikes you as 'wicked' so 'incredibly stupid,' and somehow menacing. ("How could this have ever happened?" "Can't anybody see that this crap is leading to disaster, a disaster that will roll up on this society's doorstep?" "Why can't we stop this oncoming catastrophe?") The personal nature of this issue reveals that for you it is a threat. This is your survival awareness system kick starting your probing curiosity. Allow this. Let the personal, relevant awareness activate your curiosity syndrome.

[xxviii] There is an appendage at the end where I draft examples for the non-student, the typical individual caught in the day-today economic struggle of living. Through the several illustrations, we can see how the working individual, as opposed to the full-time student, might go about the practical process of raising consciousness.

The moment this curiosity syndrome kicks in you have entered into personal change. Curiosity is a dialogue between the inner you and the outer world. Asking questions of the outer word changes how you see the world and how you sense your place in it. As we have outlined, this curiosity is a first sign of active consciousness. This consciousness through curiosity is a uniquely human attribute. Consciousness itself is transformation. The degree of consciousness speeds the changes, compounding the changes in you and how you relate to the world.

This compounding very quickly facilitates your finding that your personal irksome issue is in some way related to all the other 'troubles.' But this remains for you to uncover as consciousness compounds and expands. The first task in this 'uncovering' is to gather the tools you will need to reach out and grasp and hold this personal, irksome, and threatening issue. This remains slightly abstract. To flush out the concrete nature of the tools a concrete illustration is in order.

A Practical Example of Raising Consciousness.

Real examples from life are always helpful in grasping abstractions. For a variety of reasons I have chosen an illustration removed from the political sphere, at least overtly. The example is one that is reasonably well known and understood. At the same time the example is uniquely and immediately connected to the discussion of consciousness. I refer to the 'discovery' of the unconscious mind made by Sigmund Freud. As this example will demonstrate, the word 'discovery' is often inappropriately used. Also highlighted are the four elements of reason, curiosity, knowledge and imagination.

The example: Sigmund Freud changed forever the way in which we perceive our world. There can be very little doubt that Freud did a great deal to alter the world into which he was flung, but first he was provoked into a curiosity dialogue that altered who he was in relation to the world. How he changed himself through the curiosity syndrome and how it relates to your Situation is the next study.

Rather you consider Freud's prescription of psychoanalysis as a valid treatment for mental aberrations is beside the point. It is the illustration of a methodology for change that concerns us here, especially as it illustrates the process of 'uncovering' pathways toward affecting changing the world. 'Discovery,' as it is typically used, implies a sudden sighting (Land Ho!) or a *satori*, (sudden enlightenment, if I might borrow a concept from Zen.) Neither of these things was the case with the 'discovery' of psychoanalysis, which points out that 'discovery' is the wrong concept to apply. What the case of Freud's work does illustrate is that the uncovering and revealing process is an event that we are justified in calling 'raising con-sciousness.' Freud would likely not have described his 'discovery' in this way, but that is less important than the instruction the event of psychoanalysis has for our question, 'What Can I Do?'

The development of psychoanalytic theory was less a sudden insight, a flash of genius, than it was a lengthy and arduous process that involved the methodical application of detached reason, curiosity, prior knowledge, and the careful and judicious use of imagination. As we will see, this example of Freud's 'discovery' presents us with precisely the same structure and method any of us must use to accomplish our own goal of change.

Briefly, the facts of Freud's research and the revealing of the unconscious mind go as follows: At the age of seventeen, in 1873, Freud entered a university as a medical student. He immediately encountered the strong anti-Semitism so prevalent in the Europe of his day. There is no telling just how disturbing this encounter with anti-Semitism was for the young Freud, but it is clear that it deeply troubled him.[49] The encounter might have made Freud angry and bitter, yet he later wrote of this experience as being more puzzling than shocking. He seems to have suggested that the awareness of anti-Semitism kindled in him an attitude more akin to curiosity than hurt. His response of being puzzled and curious is telling. For it was in these early days as a medical student that Freud began to show more interest in psychology than medicine. Connecting the two – the encounter with racism and a curiosity about the workings of the mind – is in no way automatic, yet it seems entirely plausible that the anti-Semitism directed at Freud offered him an element of a personal motive to be curious about those hostile attitudes operating beyond his reach. The hostile forces that met Freud could have caused him to become enraged, or depressed and withdrawn, but the encounter did none of these things. Instead, the 'awareness of a wolf' in the vicinity made him curious. The activation of Freud's curiosity syndrome clearly would have engaged who he was in a deeper relationship with the real and threatening world around him.

The awareness of threat triggered a curiosity that reached out to the subject of mental disorders as a way that allowed Freud to uncover something about himself as inter-dependent with the world in which he was integrated. Awareness always begins with the personal, but must be fearlessly encouraged to ignite the curiosity syndrome if consciousness is to be effected in a way that permits it to be elevated. Self-change is neither effortless nor pain free. The curiosity syndrome overrode the personal and provoked an encounter with the real world in a way that allows for engagement and uncovering. In the case of Freud, curiosity opened the door to engaging the general workings of the mind. Next, we need to look into the precise nature of the engagement that led to the 'uncovering.'

From the opening of his studies, to his co-authoring a first paper on psychoanalysis, took ten years of diligent work,[50] hardly a *satori*. During this time, Freud studied with several individuals, each of whom possessed some of the keys to psychoanalysis.[51] It was though his association with each of these individuals that the dynamics of psychoanalysis were slowly revealed to Freud. This was a slow process of uncovering the many pieces of the psychoanalytic dynamic. Although it was several others who uncovered the pieces,[52] it was Freud who finally came up with the common denominator. It was Freud that took the uncovered pieces and *imaginatively* rearranged them to reveal the astonishing facts of the unconscious mind. A main truth being that certain impulses or past events were suppressed and the symptoms of hysteria (e.g. neurosis) appear as substitutes for these impulses. Today, we take much of this understanding of the unconscious mind for granted, but at the time psychoanalytic theory was a revolutionary achievement, and one, we must add, that was stubbornly resisted.

What can we learn from Freud's experience? First, it seems clear that personal motives must be present to activate and energize the curiosity syndrome. Some element of the world as perceived must have a discriminating personal hook. It is not farfetched to suggest that the Freud's encounter with anti-Semitism at the university triggered the primitive instinct for survival and well-being. It was this instinct for survival and well-being in Freud that stimulated the curiosity syndrome described above. Freud is not alone in this. This survival instinct operates within us all, and leads to the same uniquely human sense of curiosity. Next Freud demonstrated all the other qualities human beings possess; he followed the reaching out by his curiosity with dispassionate reflection off his store of accumulated knowledge; he used his imagination to rearrange the pieces he had uncovered into alternative patterns until he saw the arrangements reflected in the real suffering of individual patients. Above all, he avoided phantasmal or esoteric answers in the process of his reflecting. He remained throughout objective, corporeal, and concrete in his thinking. In each step of the way, Freud changed who he was in relationship to the events he studied. Each change brought new possibilities to light, and a new dialogue with his Situation, and ultimately with a new Freud. His accomplishments demonstrate this. What does Freud's experience mean for you?

The Practical Application with Practical Details

How can we be instructed by this example? Before all else, and especially in dealing with power relations, we must let our survival instincts lead the way. We must trust these awareness instincts for survival and well-being. This is not difficult to do. After all instincts for survival are autonomic processes. However, recall that an instinct for survival is a simple, reflexive passive awareness and not a place to get stuck. The basic fact of our humanity allows us to move beyond this raw animal state. If we feel an awareness of menace, the feeling stands a very good chance of being based in something real. How we will guide the direction of this awareness is a matter of choices that are up to us. Our best guides to survival and well-being will always be curiosity, knowledge and creative imagination. That is general practical advice, but not the necessary practical details.

The Very Practical Details: Consider carefully: *What you think is happening is very probably happening.* We must trust our instincts for survival. To paraphrase Freud's 'wayward' student, Carl Jung, 'knowing' is often more than intellect. Millions of years of genetics, by tried-and-true selection, have evolved in us highly reliable instincts. Our presence here in this human form attests to the accuracy of our survival instincts.

We can and must depend on these human survival instincts to detect threats in our world. Consider, if you think you are being cheated you probably are; if you think you are being intimidated, you very probably are; if you think you are being lied to, you very probably are – if you think something is 'wrong,' it very probably is 'wrong.' *What you think is happening is very probably happening.* Don't suppress these instincts – your personal human awareness – listen to these warnings, these instincts. Your personal instincts are as reliable a guide to survival in this world of power relations as they were for our ancestors going back to the very beginning.

Next, permit curiosity as intentional focus to reach out, envelope and pry the threatening thing loose from the landscape. Pull and separate the threatening thing from the surrounding distractions and background clutter. Pull it in for reflection, bouncing and shaping it off what you already know of power and the world. If you do not yet know enough, the reflecting itself will increase your knowledge, and hence the effectiveness of your reflection will increase, and this process will proceed in a dialectical manner. You will know something about what you instinctually feel, even if you are not certain of the something. None of us can possess complete certainty. As discussed at the very start of this project, we all co-exist with some uncertainty. It is unavoidable. Yet despite some vague sense of uncertainly, we can and do proceed. You too must proceed. There is no other way to raising consciousness. Proceed despite uncertainty.

So pick an issue. There is no issue that troubles you that is mundane or trivial. As we shall see, all that troubles you is in some degree personally triggered by your instinct for survival and well-being – your awareness. So pick an issue that is personally irksome. Be it the spread of HIV, the burden of taxation, capital punishment, abortion, famine in Horn of Africa, the decriminalization of narcotics, or perhaps climate change. None of these are trite issues. It is entirely realistic for you to feel a sense of personal menace stemming from any of these issues. They are not irrelevant. Nothing you *feel* is irrelevant or out of bounds. Any of the issues you feel can occupy your thoughts and help to define you in dialectical relationship with the world. Each of these issues is threatening in its own way, though not in the same degree for everyone.

Consider climate change, for example. It may well be that you live in a wealthy, developed country, and are a member of an elite class. This seems to put you beyond the threat of any immediate impact of climate change – or does it? You are uncertain. When reflecting on what you know about climate change, you feel that vague sense of uncertainty, and perhaps a little feeling of unease. No matter the cause of climate change you have some degree of certainty that it is real and have come to know that the change will produce world wide shifts in population, mass migration, desertification, and a global short fall in both food and fresh water. Your unease is a correct reading of these changing circumstances as a threat. They bring a threatening change to your context, your Situation. You come to be conscious that wholesale climate change is a threat to the political security of your nation and therefore almost certainly a threat to your economic station in the social system. This further piques your interest, your curiosity. Now what? Where to look for the answer to the ultimate question, 'What Can I Do?'

You must first define the thing on which you would focus. After your personal sense of awareness comes the 'curiosity' that will drive you to seek knowledge –

knowledge, that vital ingredient necessary in reflection. Like Freud, you must reach out to search through and grasp what others have uncovered. If the Situation you perceive is a genuine threat, then you are not alone in the perception and someone has already done some work on the subject. This reaching out requires study and contemplation – the accumulation of experience. This is not especially difficult, but it is time consuming. Absorbing what others have uncovered increases your knowledge base and therefore increases your powers of reflection. This starts a personal search for change in the form of dialectic. With increased reflection the knowledge base will expand and develop making possible a greater reflective ability, and so on. This is changing who you are through a dialectical relationship with the subject.

But suppose that no one has done any previous work on your subject? If your subject is real, this is highly unlikely. But let us assume the highly unlikely. It is more probable that you may not know where to look. Everything *real* makes an appearance at some time, perhaps many times and many places, though the appearing itself may not be in the form you expect. For example, the ancient Greek play, *Oedipus Rex* displays and dramatizes certain elements found in the unconscious mind that waited for a later, a much later, more complete unveiling. As seen in the case of Freud's discovery of psychoanalysis, the thing curiosity has seized upon may only have lain dormant, the odd twists of human sexuality to be uncovered by imaginatively rearranging the position of those bits and pieces previously uncovered by others. You, too, might accomplish a new uncovering. Do not think this is absurd. Such things take time and work, and even if the ultimate answer eludes you the effort is never nonsensical, or unnoticed, or without reward.

At the very least, the struggle will grant you knowledge, thus change who you are, change your Situation, and put you in a much different place in the landscape.[xxix]   As you change your integration in the terrain it will reflect on who you are. This is, after all, what you are after – a change in who you are. Most often these shifts are subtle. It is like moving down a highway with road signs leading off in a multitude of directions. Struggling with your intellectual Situation will cause the highway to get broader and more scenic. You will see things from different angles, see different opportunities, be allowed different directions to travel to more distant landscapes. No matter the direction you choose to travel, it will most likely lead to further reflection, further reasoning, increased knowledge and an imaginative reshuffling of the sign posts, of the points of interest.

Changing who you are and where you are in the landscape will freshen-up your point of view and give greater power to your imagination. You can take a long look from a different angle to get a better handle on how things might look. You can give your imagination free reign and imaginatively create a new reality, a new

---

[xxix] Again, we use the phrase 'in the landscape' rather than 'on the landscape' as a reminder that we are all integrated into the landscape and not apart from it. We are not entirely free to move about as one might wish. We are restricted, like the butcher of Wittenberg cited above, to the basic strictures of time and place of our primal circumstance.

Situation that solves the problem with a new vision of how things ought to be. This will completely adjust your vision to the nature of the threat and this will lead directly and *imaginatively* to an answer to your question, 'What Can I Do?' – an answer that is best facilitated by the change in your Situation. Changing your Situation is to dramatically experience a rising consciousness.

Raising consciousness is not a quick, one stop treatment. If you are a student you have both the time and research resources at your fingertips. It is far more difficult to achieve the same consciousness once separated from these resources, especially the all-important resource of time. Even so, the process of consciousness raising can proceed whether you are a stockbroker, or advancing in a career military, or a timber worker, or operate a small business such as an independent trucker. Unlike the student it will be a more demanding process for you in the working world. You are not normally afforded that most precious of resources, *time*, so necessary to follow the lead of curiosity; and more, to have the time for reflection and imaginative realignments of abstract pieces. Yet even if your labors are directly *related* to your survival concerns, your efforts are not *guided* by your survival concerns. Guiding your concerns is by choice, and raising consciousness in every Situation can be done and must be done. [xxx]

[xxx] The above points are suggested in the abstract. All individuals do not easily grasp abstractions. Below, in the appendage, I construct four possible case studies as more concrete illustrations. The examples are constructed for individual Situations. Through individual Situations, one can often see the greater context. The illustrations are not intended as blueprints, but as practical constructions to clarify and flush out the

Conclusion.

At this point we can see that the answer to the question of 'What Can I Do?' is not nearly so daunting or complex as one might have feared. The answer emanates from the raising of consciousness which opens numerous doors, one of which will provide an individual answer to the question. This is not some vague spiritual or magical process, but a very material process that has its roots sunk deep in the animal and human instinct to survive and be well. Raising human consciousness is therefore not just universally available, but quite possibly universally *unavoidable*. We, as individuals, can only avoid answering the question 'What Can I Do?' by sacrificing human curiosity, that anxious derivative of the instinct to survive and be well. As you should be convinced by now, to avoid curiosity is to tamper your universal humanity.

However, as you also understand by now, the raising of consciousness is no mean or easy task. It requires dedication and study, but the good news is that it is not the private haven of the full time intellectual, or the gifted genius. Consciousness, as we have argued, is the natural preserve of every human. To stress: The raising of consciousness, and therefore answering the question 'What Can I Do?' is an action and event available to everyone.

Not only this, but as we have also pointed out, raising consciousness is a universal human *responsibility*. This responsibility obliges us all because the ongoing process of expanding consciousness is the single greatest

---

abstract presentations above. For any reader not fully grasping the abstractions, considering one or more of the examples constructed in the appendage are recommended.

defining characteristic of our humanness, which is to say the uniqueness of our meaning. Rooted in simple survival instinct, the expansion of consciousness is, in fact, the basis for who we are. Raising consciousness is not just a process available to everyone; the raising of consciousness is a human ability that *obliges* everyone who wishes to keep the title of human being. Every single day we go without the elevating of consciousness, we lose a bit of our humanity. This assertion rests on the sound axiom that curiosity, that driving force behind consciousness is a derivative of our instinct for survival and well-being.

All that has been said hints at the claim that raising consciousness is the most fundamental ingredient necessary for the survival of our species. If our consciousness goes ignored or flat lines, as it were, then our species flat lines. Extinction is not just for dinosaurs and the dodo, but for all creatures whose adaptive features prove inadequate to sudden change in Situation. If we are to survive as a species, then the raising of consciousness is an adaptive instrument of human survival as surly are tooth and claw. For the sake of our survival, raising consciousness and asking the question 'What Can I Do?' does beg and oblige us all for an answer. The future of our species depends on it.

This does not imply that everyone will participate in the raising of consciousness in the same degree, or be able to, but only that humanness, mine and yours, will suffer concomitant of any lack of participation. However, and without a doubt, everyone will surly face awareness and responsibility. Instinctual evolution has made awareness unavoidable, and our existence has made choice equally unavoidable. From this point it must be recognized that the world is a complex entity. It must be seen in shades of gray, not in black and white. With black and white, we have only two dots to connect. With shades of gray the pixels are nearly infinite. Connecting the dots here is as complex as the context. It takes time and study. The connecting of a complex matrix of dots is part of the raising of your consciousness. But unlike instinct, this is a learned skill, not inherited.

It is fair to conclude that raising consciousness develops, in dialectical relationship with human survival, both individual and mass. Curiosity, the immediate derivative of awareness, makes the accumulation of experience inevitable. But keep in mind that experience is not knowledge. The greatest antagonist to the conversion of experience into knowledge, and therefore the expansion of consciousness, is a decadent or calcified system of ideas (ideology) that stands as an obstacle to genuine knowledge. In the main, ideologies that hinge on phantasmal interpretations of reality such as astrology, witchcraft, fixations on a personal supreme being, or ideological doctrines that serve as a flunky for spectral constructs such as the 'national honor,' 'racial purity' or 'the invisible hand,' are all immediately suspect as detrimental to human survival. Expanded consciousness is the quickest and surest way to overcome these transcendental handicaps.

To successfully observe political events worldwide will mean to draw a link between expanded political consciousness and what, for you, would be a new theoretical framework, a new and more successful idea-system. Built on the cornerstones of curiosity, reason, knowledge and imagination, all universally available, this new expanding consciousness is a giant step forward. In regards to the raising of individual political consciousness, you will uncover the one common denominator in answering the question of who you are. The common thread might be gender, class, nationality, *et. al.* Whatever it is, it will serve in answering the question of how you got to where you are and why you stand on the idea platform you do. That is, your consciousness as your individual history, your individual meaning as provided by you and your past choices, have brought you to your current position in the landscape. To change that consciousness to better answer the question 'What Can I Do?' requires fresh questions and answers. In the process of abandoning an old idea-system through new questions and new answers, you will uncover a variety of truths from which you must choose yours, and consciously rather than unconsciously, you will give your own unique meaning to your own life. Your political consciousness and your own personal consciousness are, as the underlying theme of this project suggests, deeply interwoven.

Finally, this paper does not delve directly into raising the political consciousness in those around you – a vital project for anyone who has achieved political consciousness. This topic must wait for another paper. For this current project it is enough to realize that the steps necessary to achieve political consciousness rest on what is innately human: Trust your instinctual awareness: *What you think is happening is probably happening.* This is based on the first element of human consciousness: awareness. Therefore: (1) This awareness will lead to a curiosity syndrome. (2) Following that lead of curiosity, you must ground of all your reasoning in the real world – spiritual or phantasmatic explanation will ultimately lead in the direction of wasted time and dead ends. (3) Glean the knowledge of power relations uncovered by others – reach out and pull these previously uncovered relations into your consciousness – they are vital for a systematic warehousing and for reflection. (4) Allow the reflection to be imaginative. This is where your individual gifts come into play. As you uncover the issues, imagine how these power relations might be reshuffled and arranged for a different agenda, an agenda friendlier to human survival and the human Situation. Here you must trust your instinct for imagination. In this case, *What you imagine can happen, can happen.* Finally, and always running in the background, you must possess the recognition that there is no final consciousness, only the ongoing process that is the unlimited raising of human consciousness. *Humanness* has no inherent limitations.

Appendage: Case Studies as Illustration.

For individuals in the work-world, time and energy are serious considerations. Still, very real things happen to you in that world, things that daily threaten your economic well-being, if not your outright survival.   Raising consciousness is a way to both understand and protect you from the hazards of that day-to-day grind. As was stated in the preface, this work is very much a how-to book. The following illustrations are a means to give you a how-to leg up for climbing the ladder of consciousness.

Case Study One: You are a timber worker in an Oregon lumber mill. The work is getting slow. You are now down to half time. This cuts deep into your pay-check, but there is no let-up in the outward flow of cash. In fact, your personal costs are increasing.   You feel yourself moving backwards. The life you have known is slipping away.   The sense of your Situation seems to be that everything is out of balance, thus increasing your feeling of vulnerability.   Anxiety and frustration set in as your economic circumstance deteriorates. You want to lash out, protect yourself. But in which direction do you strike? Is blind anger the best response?   Show fury at whom, or at what? What is the best way to deal with the change, and what is the best way to cause the change to work in the direction of balance and away from vulnerability?

What can you do? Curiosity demands a response. 'What Can I Do?' This question will arise again and again. To answer you must first uncover the reasons for your sudden change in circumstance? To take whatever kind of action you will eventually feel you must take requires answers to your change of circumstance. There are some hazy elements in your mind, but are these the key elements critical to the circumstance of the lumber industry as it relates to your personal historical Situation? Is it the environmentalists and the liberal politicians that back them? Why is it, exactly, that lumber is actually cheaper for developers to import from Asia? Yes, housing starts are off. But why is it that bank lending is down? This all seems related to who gets what, how much of it they get, and when do they get it, that is, your personal woes are bound to politics. Even so, or perhaps because of this, there are many dots to connect. Ah, it would be so simple if there were just a simple right and wrong – only two dots – but the world is a complicate place, many shades of gray, many pixels, and many dots. How to connect them?

Environmentalism, globalization, international trade, banking and lending practices, all these topics are sweeping in their scope. For a timber worker an education in economics and politics seems far-fetched. It is a hard path to take, but then the raising of consciousness is never easy. Your first step is to find sources for reliable and trustworthy help. Colleges? Universities? That is foreign terrain to you and looks too esoteric a route to take. It is not completely out of the question, but for you, intimidating and uncomfortable. There is another route.

If your workplace is unionized, the union might be a place to start. Union business agents have been compelled by their Situation to educate themselves. In order to do their job as your representative vis-à-vis the timber industry these agents had to learn a great many things directly related to you and your Situation. They can start you in the right direction by recommending literature or web sites.

Only what if your work place is not unionized, where then can you turn? The Internet is a good place. First look into the meridian uses and abuses for timber. Where this leads may surprise you, for timber is used in systems not readily grasped. This will lead you into a study of everything from the Federal Reserve to congressional committees and sub-committees on such things as environmental protection, tariff protection, banking, and the stock market. This will shortly lead to a study of the government, that confusing face of politics.

Approaching a study of these subjects is time consuming, in fact a daunting task, a task so overwhelming that few can see themselves as possessing the wherewithal to undertake the journey. This is the journey that will change who you are, change your Situation, your position in the landscape. To answer the question, 'What Can I Do?' it must be started. For the lumber worker, as for everyone else, the raising of consciousness is crucial for survival.

*** *** *** ***

Case Study Two: You are career military. War is your vocation. Only your current assignment is decidedly not business as usual. You have been sent to police a far off nation. There are immediate problems with your Situation. War has few rules. Policing is a welter of rules. You sense that something is not quite right. There seems to be a conflict between your career and your assignment. They are out of balance. The easy symmetry of our life is missing. You feel misplaced. Every day you are here, as a part of the occupation force, heightens that sense that something is wrong.

You carry your weapon into houses – huts really, dirt floors, no toilets or running water – and search for people and arms. You look at the big eyes of the women and children and you wonder, is this before you the enemy? Is the 'enemy' here, right now, and right in front to of you? You look again and awareness kicks in. You are aware that something feels not quite right. That sense of symmetry and balance is missing. This was not what you trained for. You never signed up to govern and police the activities of a general population in an occupied land. It is a task that sometimes requires you to manhandle and disrupt the lives of entire families, women, children and the elderly. This is not the bargain you made with your government. Soldiering and policing are far different occupations. Yes, you decide, there is something wrong. Remember, what you *think* is happening is very probably happening. So trust your awareness instincts and get curious. This will rally the question: Who are you and what *are* you doing here? There is no more intimate, existential question regarding who you are than this question.

Awareness first, then curiosity, and then a budding consciousness grips you. But to fully raise your consciousness to the level necessary to grasp your immediate situation you need the history of both your military and the history of this place. At some point you will uncover the old saw that this war, like all wars, is, to borrow a phrase, a "continuation of politics by other means."[53] Therefore, because politics by other means is the business of the warrior, this new awareness will lead to a direct study of your nation's politics. To fully understand why you are here in this place, doing the job of an occupying police force, you, the warrior, must raise your political consciousness through the acquisition of new knowledge of political relations in general, and the political relations of your nation in particular. This raising of your political consciousness is the most direct route to revealing who you are and what you can do.

*** *** *** ***

Case Study Three: You are in an independent trucker. You are proud to be an owner operator, a small businessman, that independent capitalist who is beholden to no one. Only you have come lately to have nagging doubts. Ironically, your Situation seems to grow less independent with each growth in business. The hauling and drayage contracts you must sign to stay in business actually confine and restrict your economic maneuverability. The contracts are less and less favorable to your business. The drayage brokers offer only long term contracts, which do not take into account rising fuel costs and weather delays. The brokers must have the stability of the contracts, and you must have the flexibility of fluid costs accounting. There seems to be no one at fault. Everyone, individually, appears trapped by the economic context in which they find themselves.

You feel hemmed in by everything from fuel prices to wicked winters. You begin to sense that your in-dependence is an illusion and that your labor is dancing to a tune played by forces beyond your control. When things go really bad you cannot cut labor costs by laying-off employees. You are the only employee. Perhaps it is your homegrown paranoia and frustration speaking. Or perhaps it is true and unavoidable in your specific Situation, something you must adjust too. But you to release yourself from the frustration you need to uncover the reality of your situation.

In your Situation, your work 'day' affords you plenty of time to think and reflect. You can certainly drive and chew gum at the same time. Time as a resource is not the issue. The issue is finding what others have already un-covered. Where to look? You have an accounting firm to handle much of your business. You might discuss your anxiety with your accountant or business manager. These are people of background and have experience in wide-ranging fields. They see the problems you face across a broad range of activities. If they cannot resolve your anxiety they can certainly direct you to sources that can expand your understanding of the economic situation you face.

Newspapers, on line journals, magazines, are other sources. Start with magazines tailored to your industry. Google 'magazine for the trucking industry', and dozens will pop up. These writers write for you and your problems. These sources are an excellent place to start. Gathering new experience requires work, but in the end it will change who you are and will change your Situation, allow you a clearer way to the answer for 'What Can I Do?'

*** *** *** ***

Case Study Four: You are a thirty-something, African-American working in a mid-level position at a stock brokerage firm in New York City. You are finding it difficult to get ahead, to make advancement in the firm. Is it racism, is it the old-boy network, have you offended the powers-that-be in some unknown way, or is it something else, something you cannot quite make out? Whatever it is, it is not your imaginings. What you think is happening is most likely happening. This is your alert system at work. As you sort it out you may find that it is a combination and accumulation of factors.

What is of pressing relevance in raising your political consciousness is the nature and impact of being black in contemporary New York. This is an immediate question, with the 'history' of the 'immediate' always running in the background. How do the power relations in this city (your immediate terrain) impact you as a black? How did those relations start? Where do they come from? What effect do those relations have on how well you will survive? These are very different questions than those a white (read: any other race) individual would face. The terrain is vastly different.[54] The answers to these questions will allow you negotiate the terrain more successfully, allow you to survive at a higher level. Not knowing them will leave you at the mercy of the wolves of history.

Like the student, you must start with history. Unlike the student, you do not have the luxury of time. Given this drawback, you can avail yourself of resources not available even a few years ago. There are cyber encyclopedias with a multitude of hyperlinks embedded that can make following 'leads' more accessible. Internet browsers are great with searchers on "History of African-Americans." Literally millions of sites will be summoned at a keystroke. I would suggest searching academic sites. They are less likely to be overtly biased, or axe grinding. This will take dedication, a willful dedication, but the ease with which information is available lessens the energy and time necessary to begin the process of raising consciousness. This willful dedication is ultimately fulfilling to the refrain of *What Can I Do?*

*** *** *** ***

Whatever your position, be sensitive to your awareness. Trust your feelings, your instinct for survival. They rarely disappoint. For example, do you sense, in a sudden flash of cognition, that certain avenues for parity are impeded by social circumstance, or do you sense that the claim to social resources, not to mention societal advancement, are denied to certain groups, or that unseen forces are at work behind a sudden downturn in your economic fortunes? Any flash of instinct may well be a flash of insight. Such quick and unexpected thoughts may not be your imaginings, and they may not be an accidental occurrence. It is highly probably that these 'insights' are connected to a political reality around you, the nature of which you are only unconsciously aware. This is not paranoia, rarely that, but it may not be a conspiracy either, or at least if it is a conspiracy it is a conspiracy of history rather than a plot hatched by evil doers cackling with relish over their evil deeds. What you sense may be the unformed, unstructured consciousness of people accepting the way things are as natural to the world.

You are not helpless. Trust your senses, for your sense of disquiet may be your untutored awareness that the way things are may not be the way things ought to be. A sense of balance and vulnerability, as discussed in the first part of this book, are universal senses and part of your individual daily appreciation for your life and your Situation. Your predisposition for a sense of balance and vulnerability are a fundamental source of power for you, and a broad avenue for you to realize what it is that you can do to bring about both personal and social change.

Endnotes

[1] There is a brand of *situation ethics* related to a narrow Christian doctrine developed by J. Fletcher in the 1960's. It is a theological perspective based on the appropriateness of setting aside moral precepts in certain situations in favor of Christian love. *Situational* ethics, as presented here, is based on a much wider and deeper philosophical understanding of universal human circumstance (or ontology) and is more closely related to existentialism.

[2] For greater depth see Martin Heidegger's *Being and Time*, or J.P. Sartre's *Being and Nothingness*, though the two philosophers will differ in their arguments and conclusions.

[3] Immanuel Kant, *Grounding for the Metaphysics of Morals*, various publications, .§ (448)

[4] For example, see G.E. Moore, *Philosophical Papers*, (Unwin Brothers limited, London, 1959) p. 240

[5] It remains incontrovertible that we can cast doubt on anything except that we can doubt, an original observation made by René Descartes in the 17th Century; this seems to place doubt beyond ideology.

[6] There are far more technical, philosophical treatments of truth, for example, see Paul, Moser, Mulder and Trout, *The Theory of Knowledge*, (Oxford University Press, New York, 1998), especially chapter four, "Truth."

[7] For example, for a detailed summation of this subject, see Frederick Schmitt, *Truth, A Primer*, (Westview Press, Boulder, 1995)

[8] To the professional philosopher: please note that I am conspicuously avoiding terms like *idealist* and *realist*, or *metaphysical*, for what should be obvious reasons.

[9] For example, see Charles Fried, *Right And Wrong*, (Harvard University Press, Cambridge, 1978), especially the chapter: "On Lying."

[10] Ludwig Wittgenstein, *On Certainty*, (Harper Torchbook, New York, 1972) p. 36 (sec. 282)

[11] One of the best and shortest elucidations of Darwin's life and theories can be found on line at:
http://anthro.palomar.edu/evolve/evolve_2.htmF

[12] The meaning of Being is not firmly established in philosophy. As it is used here, Being means 'how one is in relationship to their existence.' This transcends specific space and time to look at the more fundamental questions of our human foundation in this reality.

[13] For an excellent work on the major moral systems see C.D. Broad, *Five Types of Ethic Theory*, (Routledge & Kegan Paul, New York, 1971)

[14] The exception to this might be Immanuel Kant.

[15] Renford Bambrough, "Proof of the Objectivity of Morals," found in Robert Cunningham, *Situationism and the New Morality,* (Appleton-Century-Crofts, New York, 1970), pp 107-108

[16] Note that both positions advocate negative action, or at the very least inaction, i.e. to *not* burn down a house, to *not* render assistance. This prejudice against *action* in favor of *inaction* will be discussed in greater detail later as it bears strongly on our overall project.

[17] For example, see Gilbert Harman, *The Nature of Morality* (Oxford: Oxford University Press, 1977), wherein Harman strongly suggests that this cultural prejudice against an offer of assistance is part of some self-serving bargaining on the part of the wealthy and the powerful who might otherwise face extreme pressure to divest themselves of their money and power should such rendering of assistance became the norm. While the norm is self-serving, it also reverses causation as it seems counter to anthropological studies that determine that cultural ethos evolve prior to any such consciously deliberate and calculated political maneuvering.

[18] If there is any doubt about the fact that males are battered by their spouses in significant number, a Google search of "Battered Husbands" would serve to dispel the myth.

[19] An obvious and notorious case involved the assault of John Bobbitt by his wife, Lorena, in June of 1993. In response to years of abuse, claimed Lorena, including being raped by John, she cut off her husband's penis with a carving knife. There is little doubt but that issues of vulnerability and imbalance will quickly surface when considering this case.

[20] Goetz shot four youths in a New York subway car in 1984 whom were aggressively 'panhandling' money. For a lengthy elucidation see: http://en.wikipedia.org/wiki/Bernhard_Goetz

[21] There is no way to know the exact mix of the contextual understanding that motivated the jurors, but it seems highly probable that all these elements were present in their decision.

[22] For a highly detailed account of the efforts of the court to achieve a balanced jury, and prosecute the 'crime' as fully as possible, see: George Fletcher, *A Crime of Self-Defense: Bernard Goetz and The Law on Trial,* (Free Press, New York, 1988)

[23] John Cook, *Morality And Cultural Differences,* (Oxford University Press, New York, 1999) p. 94

[24] It is important to resist the idea that this represented some kind of moral relativism. It is better to see it as moral projection, rather than relativism. For an analysis of moral projection, as opposed to moral relativism, see Steven Lukes, *Moral Relativism,* (St. Martin's Press, New York, 2008), especially pages 70-77

[25] The word 'ontology' should not be as intimidating as it has become. It has become very complex, and is frequently used as a synonym (incorrectly, I believe) for metaphysics, which is to say a thing rising above the physical, temporal realm of reality. This is not the meaning of ontology as used here. As I mean ontology here it is the study of Being, which is to say: what does it *mean* that I exist as a conscious physical entity. What is the nature of human existence? There is nothing spiritual, or metaphysical, about these questions. Ontology concerns itself with our living consciousness, self-consciousness, that we intentionally reflect, etc., and what does all this ultimately mean for our existence. Our ontology is what we are as existing creatures in time and space.

[26] Soren Kierkegaard might be cited as a counter to this philosophical rejection of God, for Kierkegaard would say that only through the acceptance of (and the alignment with) God can our sense of meaningless be put to rest; our fear and angst stems from our sense of purposelessness, which, according to Kierkegaard, must be seen as the result of the rejection of God, and not caused by it. Other philosophers have rejected Kierkegaard's claim as a mere desperate bid to save purpose in the form of God.

[27] As often the responsibility picture is hidden from us, and for those needing more examples of universal connectedness, the following is offered: We can even witness the connectedness between personal choice and universal connectedness through Israeli universal conscription. These political choices by Israeli leaders concerning universal conscription clearly connect the lives of all the citizens of Israel. Likewise, submission by the individual Israeli to conscription connects that citizen to the state of Israel and all its policies (and also to the Palestinians). The state of Israel, as well as any national state, is a metaphysical entity in only the most limited of sense. More realistically, the nation state of Israel is a geographical unit made of

people who *connect* with the political dynamic of that geographical unit. With that connection to the political dynamic come consequences and responsibility. In a like manner, conscription practices by the Israeli state connect with the citizens of all the surrounding states, i.e. a stronger Israeli military emphasizes the need for a balancing strength in the surrounding states to neutralizing Israeli's military power. This, in turn, has economic and political consequences for all the citizens of the surrounding states. As a pebble tossed into a quiet pond has ripple effects the political dynamic of one national state ultimately has some consequence for the citizens of all national states. For example, we can see that these decisions have impact on weapons manufacturing in considerable number of countries. This in turn demands decisions as to the allocation of resources which greatly influences far flung societies and individuals within those societies. Choices are forced on people far removed from the original choices. The choices and responsibility have universal consequences. They have been universalized.

What of the universal effect of Bernhard Goetz? Rather we agree with the criminal verdict, or the ethical implications, we must admit that it has had an impact on the way prosecutors and defense attorneys come to handle similar situations, and certainly the knowledge of the situation has strengthened juries to raise claims that rise above the law. In short, the Goetz case has weakened the automatic criminal reflex and strengthened some extra-legal understanding of social rules and procedures. In a manner of speaking it has given increased license for juries to step outside of the normal legal rulings to find juridical rulings. This may have been partial result of an earlier jury decision regarding the assassination of Harvey Milk and George Moscone, often referred to as the "Twinkie Defense."

[The term "Twinkie Defense" was coined by a reporter. It mischaracterized the defense tactic of diminished capacity as a factor in the murders. In the defense of Dan White, the defense lawyers never mentioned Twinkies or claimed that a sugar rush led to the killings of Moscone and Milk. The claim of the defense lawyers was that junk food was a symptom of White's state of mind, his diminished capacity.]

The ways in which nation states respond to the demands of history have widespread implications. Both the leaders of those states and the people at large bear some responsibility for the effects of their choices. Likewise, the Goetz case opened the door for unique defense strategies that permanently altered the legal landscape. Thus the responsibility for this altered legal landscape resides universally with all individuals who offer support to the Anglo-Saxon judicial system.

[28] Machiavelli comes to mind as the obvious manipulator of ideology *qua* doctrine.

[29] Sartre might say that in choosing to recognize the freedom to choose, he has chosen to be human and therefore he has chosen 'human,' with the universal connectedness that implies. For Kant, to be human is to possess reason. Through the universality of reason we possess a universal obligation to practice reason. Since reason is a natural 'obligation' to every human being, every human being is the origin of that universality and by reason is connected to the universality of humanness and all humans.

[30] For a lengthy contrast of the two, awareness and consciousness, see: William G. Lycan, *Consciousness*, (MIT Press, Cambridge, MA, 1987).

[31] See: Nelkin Norton, *Consciousness and the Origin of Thought*, (Cambridge University Press, Cambridge, MA 1996).

[32] See: Daniel Dennett, *Content and Consciousness*, (Routledge and Keagan, London, 1993).

[33] For a somewhat extended treatment of this topic see: Charles Fried, *Right and Wrong*, (Harvard University Press, Cambridge, 1978), especially pp. 22-28

[34] For an excellent overview of the Jovian moon, Europa, see: http://www.solarviews.com/eng/europa.htm

[35] Space and time prevent me from going into the subject of time in any detail. However, our understanding of time may well be related to our abstract grasp of our own death, but it is beyond the scope of this paper to explore this dimension. Other philosophers, such as Martin Heidegger, have rather interesting and lengthy discussions of the subject.

[36] We should note, if only as an aside, that the meaning revealed by the re-arrangement of patterns must either be compatible with a prevailing ideology, or a breakout from ideological restrictions.

[37] The more conventional view, that language is the most important tool in the controls ideas can be found in such as Daniel Dennett, *Kinds of Minds*, (Basic Books, New York, 1996), pp. 146, 147; the considerably more complex argument, that ideology dominates language, is one worked extensively by Jurgen Habermas, for elucidation, see David McLellan's *Ideology*, (University of Minnesota Press, Minneapolis, 1986) pp. 77, 78

[38] Again, time and space prevents a detailed discussion, but 'Will' may be a manifestation of desire, if I may follow Arthur Schopenhauer's suggestion, and thereby give will a possible origin in human biological

drives. However, for the purposes of this paper it is only important to note that will and intention are a basic part of the human makeup.

[39] We do not know if Thales predicted a total or partial eclipse. Predicting a total eclipse would have been far more technically impressive.

[40] While many philosophers will disagree with me, I tend to house metaphysical systems under the same roof as superstition. The reader is cautioned not to confuse abstract explanations with metaphysics.

[41] As Nietzsche so keenly observed, curiosity led to the death of God, which goes a long way to explaining why St. Augustine thought that curiosity was a deadly sin.

[42] As a pre-Socratic, little is known of the education of Thales. It is known, however, that he was from a patrician, Phoenician family. These families paid great attention to the education of their children, and Thales no doubt had the best tutors available. We know that he did receive his mathematical education from Egyptian priests whose interest in astronomy is well known. It is from them that he might have learned of solar eclipses, and some sense of how to predict them.

[43] There have been both left and right wing attempts to describe anarchy in practice. For example, on the left see Samuel Clark, *Living Without Domination*, (Ashgate, Hampshire, GB, 2007); on the right see Robert Nozick, *Anarchy, State, and Utopia*, (Basic Books, New York, 1977).

[44] See: Jurgen Habermas, *Towards A Rational Society*, (Beacon Press, Boston, 1970)

[45] This is not to suggest that resignation reigned supreme. For example, see Howard Zinn, *A People's History of the United States* (Harper Perennial, Modern Classics, New York, 2003), especially chapters 13,14, & 15; or see Philip Foner, *A History of the Labor Movement in the United States*, (International Publishers, New York, 1964) especially, Vol. 3

[46] For a early and lengthy treatment of this alienating process, see: Herbert Marcuse, *One Dimensional Man*, (Beacon Press, Boston, 1964)

[47] For those interested in a short exploration of ontology and its implications you might get a better understanding by following some types of ontological arguments. There are several such arguments and articles to be found in the on-line edition of the Stanford Encyclopedia of Philosophy. For example, one might wish to look into ontological arguments surrounding the existence of God. In that case, see: http://plato.stanford.edu/entries/ontological-arguments/

[48] There is an interesting book by Hurbert Dreyfus that explores this theme through the work of Martin Heidegger, Hurbert Dreyfus, *Being-In-The-World*, (MIT Press, Cambridge, 1991).

[49] For a highly readable elucidation of Freud's life and work the biography by Ernest Jones is highly recommended. Jones, Ernest, *The Life and Work of Sigmund Freud*, abridged version by L Trilling and S. Marcus (London: Penguin, 1964; Basic Books, 1961)

[50] Freud first published a joint paper on the subject with Josef Breuer in 1893.

[51] For example, Freud studied with the Frenchman Charcot and witnessed the effects of hypnosis as a relief for maladies then called 'hysteria.' Later, through an association with Josef Breuer, Freud learned that through verbal expression, the revealing of some connection between symptoms and past events was possible. Through the verbalizing of the connection, the subject could be relieved of the symptoms. It was at this point that Freud made the common connection that some forgotten event or impulse was suppressed by certain outside factors; this suppression caused the symptoms to appear as a substitute for the act or a twisted version of the original event.

[52] To his credit Freud always gave acknowledgement to others (especially to Josef Breuer) for their significant contributions to his findings.

[53] Carl von Clausewitz

[54] This does not imply that a black individual cannot have an understanding of white conditions, or vice-versa, but only that the historical position of the two races dramatically affects the terrain, a landscape that is unique to each race and spells the difference between understanding and consciousness.

Index

Kant, Immanuel, 15, 100, 201-204, en 14, 29
Kevorkian, Jack, 62
Kierkegarrd, Soren, 65, 201, en 26

Lydians, 129, 130

Machiavelli, 167, 161, fn, 202 en 28
Malthusian, 107
Mass media, 157
Medians, 129, 130
Mexico, 155

Nationalism, 151, 159, 189
Nazis, 49, 70, 86, 87
Nietzsche, Frederic, 204, en, 39
Nihilism, 45, 54

Oedipus Rex, 183
Ontological puzzlement, 120

Patriotism, 151, 159, 160
Polygamy, 44
Psychoanalysis, 176, 178, 183

Racism, 149, 150, 177, 197
Republican Party, 106
Rights of property, 48
Russia, 155

Sartre, 100, 200 en, 2, 204 en, 24
Schopenhauer, Arthur, 204 en, 36
Sisyphus, the myth of, 69
Socialism, 106
South Africa, 149
Spartacus, 83 fn

Tehrani, Mahnaz, (martyr) 83 fn
Thales of Miletus, 129-131, 134, 135, 159,
204-205 en, 37, 40
The Stranger, 78
Torture, 68, 82, 83, 83 fn
Treaty of Versailles, 49
Turner, Nat, 83 fn

Voltaire, 104

Wittgenstein, Ludwig, 31, 33
World War Two, 49

Xenophobia, 149,159

Zen, 176
Zyklon B, 87

BIBILOGRAPHY

Anderson, Thomas. *The Foundations and Structure of Sartrean Ethics*. (Lawrence, KS: Regents Press of Kansas, 1979)

Aristotle. *The Nicomachean Ethics*. Translated by David Ross. (Oxford: Oxford University Press, 1998)

Aristotle. *The Politics of Aristotle*. Translated by B. Jowett. (Oxford, UK: The Clarendon Press, 1885)

Bambrough, Renford, "Proof of the Objectivity of Morals," found in Robert Cunningham, *Situationism and the New Morality* (Appleton-Century-Crofts, New York, 1970)

Barnes, Hazel. *An Existentialist Ethics*. (New York: Alfred A. Knopf, 1967)

Beauchamp, Tom. *Philosophical Ethics, An Introduction to Moral Philosophy*. (New York: McGraw Hill, 1982)

Broad, C.D., *Five Types of Ethic Theory*, (Routledge & Kegan Paul, New York, 1971)

Brown, Montague. *The Quest for Moral Foundations*. (Washington D.C.: Georgetown University Press, 1996)

Chomsky, Noam. *Profit Over People*. (New York, NY: The Seven Stories Press, 2000)

Cook, John, *Morality And Cultural Differences*, (New York: Oxford University Press, 1999)

De Beauvoir, Simone. *The Ethics of Ambiguity*. Translated by Bernard Frechtman, (New York: Citadel Press, 1967)

Dennett, Daniel. *Content and Consciousness*. (London: Routledge and Kegan Paul, 1993)

Finley, M.I. *The World of Odysseus*. (New York: New
York Review Books, 2002)

Foner, Philip. *A History of the Labor Movement in the
United States* (New York: International Publishers,1964)

Foot, Philippa. *Natural Goodness*. (Oxford: The
Clarendon Press, 2001)

Fried, Charles, *Right And Wrong*, (Cambridge: Harvard
University Press, 1961)

Glover, Jonathan. *Humanity, A Moral History of the
Twentieth Century*, (New Haven: Yale University Press,
1999)

Gurtler, Gary. "The Activity of Happiness." *The Review of
Metaphysics*, 55, no. 4 (2000)

Habermas, Jurgen, *Towards A Rational Society*, (Boston,
Beacon Press, 1970)

Harman, Gilbert, *The Nature of Morality* (Oxford: Oxford
University 1978)

Heidegger, Martin. *Introduction to Metaphysics*.
Translated by G. Fried and R. Polt. (New Haven: Yale
University Press, 2000)

Heidegger, Martin. *The Question Concerning Technology
andOther Essays*, Translated by William Lovitt. (New
York:Harper and Row, 1977)

Howells, Christina, ed. *The Cambridge Companion to
Sartre* (Cambridge, UK: Cambridge University Press,
1992)

Hurbert Dreyfus, *Being-In-The-World*, (Cambridge: MIT
Press, 1991)

Immanuel Kant. *Grounding for the Metaphysics of Morals*,
various publications

Jones, Ernest. *The Life and Work of Sigmund Freud*,
Abridged version L Trilling and S. Marcus (London:
Penguin, 1964; Basic Books, 1961)

Kockelmans, Joseph, *Contemporary European Ethics*.
(New York: Anchor Books, 1972)

Levi, Primo. *Survival in Auschwitz*. Translated by Stuart
Woolf, (New York:Tourchstone Books, 1996)

Lukes, Steven, *Moral Relativism*, (New York: St. Martins
Press, 2008)

Lycan, William G., *Consciousness*, (Cambridge: MIT Press,
1987)

Manser, Anthony. *Sartre, A Philosophical Study*. (Oxford:
Oxford University Press, 1966)

Marcuse, Herbert. *One Dimensional Man*, (Boston: Beacon
Press, 1964)

Matson, Wallace. *A New History of Philosophy*. (New York:
Harcourt Brace, 1987)

May, Rollo._*The Discovery Of Being*. (New York: W.W.
Norton & Co., 1983)

McBride, William. *Existentialist Ethics*. (New York:
Taylor and Francis, 1996)

Montesquieu, Charles-Louis *The Spirit Of The Laws*.
Translated by Franz Newmann. (New York: Hafner
Publishing Co, 1959)

Montesquieu, Charles-Louis. *The Spirit of the Laws*
Translatedby Anne M. Cohler, (New York: Cambridge
University Press, 1989)

Moore, G.E. *Philosophical Papers*, (Unwin Brothers
Limited, London, 1959)

Moran, Dermot. *Introduction to Phenomenology*. (New
York: Routledge, 2000)

Moser, Paul, Mulder and Trout, *The Theory of Knowledge*,
(New York: Oxford University Press, 1998)

Nagel, Thomas, *The View From Nowhere*. (Oxford: Oxford
University Press, 1986)

Norton, Nelkin, *Consciousness and the Origin of Thought*,
(Cambridge: Cambridge University Press, 1977)

Robertson, R. *Globalization*, (Boston: Sage Publications,
2004)

Sartre, J.P. *Being and Nothingness*. Translated by Hazel
    Barnes. (New York: Philosophical Library, 1956)
Sartre, J.P. *Truth and Existence*. Translated by Adrian
    Van den Hoven. Edited by Ronald Aronson. (Chicago:
    University of Chicago Press, 1992)
Sartre, J.P. "Interview with Jacqueline Piatier." *Le Monde*,
    April 18, 1964.
Sartre, J.P. "The Humanism of Existentialism." In *Essays
    In Existentialism*, (Secaucus, NJ, The Citadel Press, 1972)
Sartre, J.P. *Notebooks For An Ethics*. Translate by David
    Pellauer. (Chicago: University of Chicago Press, 1992)
Scanlon, T.M. *What We Owe To Each Other* (Cambridge,
    MA: Belknap Press, 1989)
Schmitt, Fredrick, *Truth, A Primer*, (Boulder: Westview
    Press,1995)
Schopenhauer, Arthur. *Philosophy of Arthur Schopenhauer*
    Translated by Belfort Bax and Bailey Saunders. (New
    York:Tudor Publishing Co., 1946)
Scott, Nathan. *Mirrors of Man in Existentialism*.
    (Cleveland,OH: William Collins and World Publishing,
    1978)
Simon, Yves. *The Definition of Moral Virtue*. (New York:
    Fordham University Press, 1986)
Vattimo, Gianni. *The End of Modernity*. Translated by Jon
    Snyder. (Baltimore: Johns Hopkins University Press,
    1991)
Von Clausewitz, Carl. *On War*. Edited and translated by M.
    Howard and P. Paret. (New York: Everyman's Library,
    Alfred Knopf, 1993)
Wittgenstein, Ludwig. *On Certainty*, (Harper Torchbook,
    New York, 1972)
Zinn, Howard. *A People's History of the United States*
    (New York: Harper Perennial Modern Classics, 2003)

Made in the USA
Charleston, SC
03 March 2012